THER.   .OOM
Three Performance Texts

THERE'S A ROOM
Three Performance Texts

WHERE FROM HERE
Third Angel
Rachael Walton
Jerry Killick
Alexander Kelly

PRESUMPTION
Third Angel
Alexander Kelly
Chris Thorpe
Rachael Walton

WHAT I HEARD ABOUT THE WORLD
Third Angel & mala voadora
Jorge Andrade
Alexander Kelly
Chris Thorpe
with
José Capela
Rachael Walton

OBERON BOOKS
LONDON

WWW.OBERONBOOKS.COM

First published in 2019 by Oberon Books Ltd
521 Caledonian Road, London N7 9RH
Tel: +44 (0) 20 7607 3637 / Fax: +44 (0) 20 7607 3629
e-mail: info@oberonbooks.com
www.oberonbooks.com

PB ISBN: 9781786827524
E ISBN: 9781786827500

Cover: Third Angel's *Where From Here*, photo by Rob Hardy

Visit www.oberonbooks.com to read more about all our books and to buy them. You will also find features, author interviews and news of any author events, and you can sign up for e-newsletters and be the first to hear about our new releases.

Printed on FSC® accredited paper

10 9 8 7 6 5 4 3 2 1

Contents

'Who's in the room?' This is the question we ask ourselves about each project. It means, who is making this show? Who is in the room in which the work is getting made? Whose voices, whose expertise, whose experience is being brought together to tell this story with us?

Where From Here was made in Sheffield Independent Film's studio, on Brown Street, in the autumn of 2000. *Presumption* was made in Dead Earnest Theatre Company's rehearsal room, at The Quadrant, just off Sheffield's Parkway, early 2006. *What I Heard About the World* was made through a more extended process during 2010, in our studio in Brookfield Yard, and Sheffield Theatres' rehearsal rooms in the Crucible and then Lyceum Theatres. These, on the one hand, are the rooms referred to in the title of this collection. Whilst presented here as scripts ready to be performed, these three shows were all created through group devising processes, specific to the time, place and group of individuals gathered together to make them.

Every devising process is unique, of course, but ours will often draw from the same box of tools for writing – or 'generating text' as we often refer to it. We record improvised conversations, transcribe and edit them. We stand up and improvise the same speech repeatedly, honing it, with one of us in the outside-eye or director role, giving feedback. We come up with rules that govern what a performer might say in a particular section, without ever fixing it from one performance to the next. We all sit down at a laptop or notebook and write a draft of a speech or a scene, and come back together after an hour and share what we have. We bring in sections of text that we have come up with at home overnight.

These sections are usually tried out and developed without us knowing exactly where in the show they will fit. We create the bricks and then start to build the show out of them. Some are discarded along the way; others, when placed together, reveal gaps that need to be filled. As the structure of the show begins to take shape, the separate texts are revisited, so that they sit well in context, in relation to each other, as part of the show as a whole. At some point they are presented to an audience, and we learn new things about what we have made. Sections evolve, running orders are rejigged. Some improvised sections settle on something like a final text. Others, we might realise, will always need to be of the moment, worded slightly differently every time. The performance texts collected here represent each show fairly late on in their touring lives, after many of these discoveries have been made.

The title of this collection also refers to the situation of each show, and the concerns of the work. Each takes place in a particular room – in which the audience are acknowledged to a greater or lesser extent. In each piece the lives of the people in the room together are affected by events in the world beyond its walls. Events they have taken part in, events they have heard about, events they have imagined. Taken chronologically, the three shows turn their attention outward, from the intensity of personal relationships and our domestic lives, to the overwhelming number of stories and events taking place in the world beyond.

Our thanks go to the whole Oberon team for their patience in making this collection happen, and to you for reading. We hope you enjoy the work.

Rachael Walton & Alexander Kelly
Sheffield, September 2019

Jerry Killick in *Where From Here* publicity shot. Photo: Rob Hardy.

WHERE FROM HERE

Performance text by
Rachael Walton
Jerry Killick
Alexander Kelly

Close Your Eyes

Where From Here was something of a coming-of-age project for Third Angel. We came in to the making process for the show at the end of the summer of 2000 with a clear collection of starting points, and a strong sense of what the show was about.

Back in 1998 we had made a durational performance called *Senseless* for Arnolfini in Bristol and The Mappin Gallery in Sheffield. Three performers, blindfolded for three, 10-hour days.[1] One of the tasks the performers had was to remember, describe, and draw every room they had ever lived in. This was a surprisingly satisfying performative task to watch, particularly as the audience were up close with the performers, separated only by transparent plastic walls.[2] It was enjoyable, and sometimes moving, to watch people remembering, to watch them concentrating on their task. The drawings they made, floor plans with not-to-scale furniture, books and ornaments spilling out beyond the walls, were fascinating. Beautiful even. It worked well as a durational, autobiographical performance task, but we had a sense that it could also be a mechanism for more constructed, fictional, storytelling.

We were interested in how people could remember the same event differently – and how those different memories of the same situation might then affect their relationship. We had set out to make a 'relationship show' a couple of times before. But in early 1997 the domesticity of a show idea called *Burning The Toast* somehow transformed itself into an escapist sci-fi thriller *Experiment Zero*.

1   In Bristol; in Sheffield four of us alternated over five, 6-hour days.

2   For more about *Senseless* see www.thirdangel.co.uk/shows-projects/senseless

In 1998 *Saved* had gone from being a filmic two-hander to a much more insular one-sided story of the life of a relationship.

At the start of 2000 we had thought we might make a show called *Stranger Danger*, about the perils of falling in love, or of getting too close to other people. This time we wanted to tell the story of a relationship from both sides at the same time, to explore the complexity of emotions in a close relationship. The pitch document for that show contained the line 'everything that is wrong in the world is somebody else's fault.'

Early that year we had a week-long residency at the ICA in London. We wanted to try to bring these ideas together in a show about happiness. About what, and who, makes us happy. We made a video of Rachael 'being happy' for an hour. A mid-shot of her sitting on a chair, thinking about things that made her happy, and smiling. There was something enjoyably weird about it, and it reassured us that this was the territory we wanted to explore.

Over the summer of 2000 we collaborated with German company Drei Wolken to make *The Secret Hippie Piece*, a show for the top deck of a multi-story car park in Hildesheim[3] which attempted to ask, in part, how do we try to be happy in the modern world? In the city? What choices do we make, and why? This multi-stranded project produced a great deal of material, and, as with many devising processes, not all of it was used. We brought home with us a couple of sections of text about happiness that had been thought too personal for *The Secret Hippie Piece*, that we thought might guide us into making what we were now calling *Where From Here*.[4]

3   And later Frankfurt and Gießen.
4   Without a question mark. We had a meeting about it.

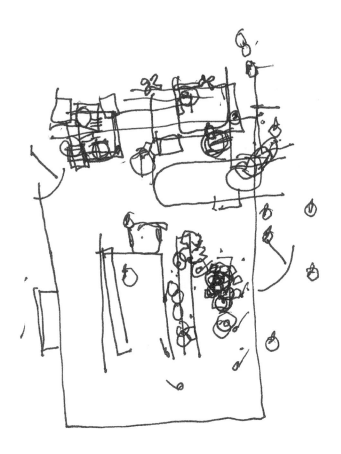

We had designed and ordered an all-white set consisting of three walls and a floor, with two doors and a 'secret' cupboard. It was all white, and (in theory) wipe-clean, to allow us to draw on to the walls, and also to project video onto it. Much of our previous work had involved the use of film and video, and this was something that – it seemed to us at least – was an identifiable characteristic of Third Angel's work. We thought we would develop that element further.

We had met deviser/performer Jerry Killick, and seen his work, whilst he was making *Who Can Sing A Song To Unfrighten Me?* with Forced Entertainment the previous year. We had many of the same references and felt like we could work well together, and happily this proved to be the case.

Staging Happiness

We never really got around to projecting onto the white walls. We certainly did not make any film or video work. As soon as we started drawing on the walls of the room, right from the outset, we realised that this was both the aesthetic and the mechanism of the show. A structure emerged in which the performer/characters would remember a room, and draw it on the walls of the set, and then tell a story from their relationship, something that happened in that room. The performers, Rachael and Jerry, co-opted real, remembered places as the setting for fictionalised events from an imagined relationship. The rule seemed to be that the white room, with its single table and two chairs, would 'become' the drawn room, until another was remembered and described. This collection of rooms, and stories set in them, would tell the story of their relationship. The highs and the lows.

A couple of weeks into the making process we realised that we had the couple getting together, experiencing doubt, breaking up (not told in that order, of course). But we didn't have them *being happy* together. So we gave ourselves the task of finding a room, and a story, where we could spend time with them, being happy. We had them hanging out together. A surprise birthday cake. Candles.

It was awful.

Rachael and Jerry did a good job of them being happy. That was partly the problem. It felt too private; there was something about it that excluded the audience. When we tried to turn it out from the stage more, it felt smug. It is, arguably, what many of us want: to simply be happy with someone. But of course dramatically, theatrically, there's nothing at stake. Much more enjoyable was the nervous risk of them getting together after a dinner party – with the potential of happiness in the air. We accepted that the getting together scene, told by the two of them, showing them working well together, making each other laugh, would do the job of showing them happy.

Multiple Outputs

Alongside this we were playing with material that branched off from the room-story structure of the show. Distractions, perhaps, from the relationship. Brief moments where the couple would give voice to momentary anger, and imagine deliberately, physically hurting each other. That secret cupboard was behind a built-in display cabinet for their weapons, which they would each return to from time to time. They rearranged the furniture.[5] They took hobbies and board games far too seriously. They noticed that everyone around them had taken up running. They admitted to lying to each other. A strand emerged where the two of them would explain these digressions, making their case to the audience, as if to a jury, as to why they were right. Why it was not their fault.

For one of these sections we began playing with a list of imagined pharmaceuticals, which we began to refer to as *Pills For Modern Living*. Convenient, apparently magical, pills that could solve your day-to-day problems. A *Tip of the Tongue Pill*. A *Not My Problem Pill*. A *Heart Mended Pill*. These were the only things we tried projecting on to the white walls – brightly coloured diagrams of the pills themselves. But in the end that did not seem in keeping with the hand drawn aesthetic, and we preferred to see and hear the pills rattling in their plastic bottles.

---

5   Giving shape to a performative obsession that would arguably find its zenith in *Presumption* six years later.

But we liked the images, and realised that this idea could work in a number of frames – that one process could result in multiple outputs. The *Pills For Modern Living* became a series of lightboxes that could be exhibited in galleries or found spaces.[6] This in turn inspired a series of commemorative postcards and then a short film, combining the images and the speech from the show, *Pills 03:30:00*. This realisation that a 'single' process could produce multiple outputs in different forms would go on to influence much of our work in the years that followed, with a number of extended research processes that branched out into several related performances and projects.

6   First up was a Victorian public toilets in Bristol in collaboration with the In Between Time Festival.

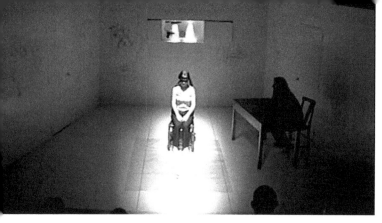

Rachael Walton and Jerry Killick in *Where From Here*.
Screengrabs by Christopher Hall.

Friday Afternoons

Where From Here was made over six weeks
in the Studio at Sheffield Independent Film. On
Friday afternoons we would be joined by as
many of the team as were around, including
lighting designer James Harrison, composer Lee
Sykes and General Manager Hilary Foster, plus,
occasionally, friends invited in to give feedback.
We would present them with as much material
as we had, and then discuss what was working,
what else we needed, where we would go next.
Everyone had licence to chip in on all aspects of
the production – not just their own area.

One of these Friday afternoons, Lee played
us some music, and we talked about what we
were interested in, how we thought the music
could work in the show. There was a moment
of realisation. 'Oh,' Lee said, 'you don't want a
theatre soundtrack, you want a film score.'
It was so obvious when articulated like that – so
obvious to us that we had not thought to mention
it. But it reminded us that just because something
is instinctive to one or more of us, you cannot as-
sume that it is obvious for everyone.

Touring

Where From Here opened at The Roadmender, Northampton, on 6 November 2000. It toured in the UK through into spring 2001, followed by performances in Frankfurt. After these gigs we revised the ending, making it slightly more ambiguous, and taking out a final gag that undercut the melancholy of the last scene. It is this second version that is published here. In August 2001 we took the show to the Edinburgh Festival Fringe (with Alex stepping into Jerry's role for some of these performances) as part of the British Council's Edinburgh Showcase. This led to performances in Budapest, Lisbon, Mannheim and Brussels along with several international creative learning projects, which in turn had a great impact on our practice over the following years.

Rachael Walton in *Where From Here* publicity shot. Photo: Rob Hardy.

Third Angel presents
WHERE FROM HERE

Devised by the company

Performed by
Jerry Killick & **Rachael Walton**
and occasionally
Alexander Kelly

Directed and Designed by
Alexander Kelly & **Rachael Walton**

Lighting Design
James Harrison

Soundtrack
Lee Sykes at Vortex Music

Set Construction
Vision Works

Dramaturgy Placement
Catherine Wilson

Administration
Phillippa Yates
Hilary Foster

Publicity Photography
Rob Hardy (targets)
Alexander Kelly (kitchen)

Pills 03:20:20 created by
Christopher Hall

Where From Here was first performed at The Roadmender, Northampton, 6 November 2000, and toured in the UK and internationally through to 2003.

Funded by the Arts Council of England, Yorkshire Arts, Sheffield City Council, the Performing Rights Society Foundation and supported by the ICA, Site Gallery and Sheffield Independent Film.

Cast

A WOMAN and a MAN, both late 20s/early 30s.

Set

A white room: three-sided with angled side walls, plus a slightly raised floor, all covered in the same white matt plastic which allows it to be used as a whiteboard, but which does not reflect light so much as to blind the audience.

The side walls consist of four flats each, and the back wall, three flats. In the third flat from the audience, in both walls, there is a door. In the middle panel in the back wall are two cupboard doors, four feet from the floor, opening into a cupboard, containing various weapons on hooks: some domestic tools (a hacksaw, pliers, claw hammer) some less ambiguous – a piece of rope, a gun. For reference, the flats are numbered 1-9 (not including the door panels) from downstage left (1) to downstage right (9). In larger performance spaces, two additional flats are added downstage right and left, square to the audience to mask backstage.

In the room: two wooden chairs and a wooden table about 4' long by 2' deep with two drawers. We use this furniture in the condition we found it – a little shabby.

Props

Toy BB gun (plus pellets), targets, carving knife, rope, Stanley knife, hacksaw, claw hammer, blindfold, old Monopoly game, bottles of pills, whiteboard pens, 4' x 4' sheet of clear polythene.

Room Drawing

Throughout the show, the two performers describe and draw plans of rooms, with their eyes closed, on the walls of the set. The original descriptions were mainly real rooms from the performers' own experience, and therefore they changed to some extent with any change in cast, or if a performer rearranged their furniture at home whilst still on tour. Similarly, the I WILL MISS section was improvised and personal to the performers.

Script and Performance

Where From Here *was devised through weeks of improvisation, exercises and experimentation. This script was compiled from memory and video documentation, and as such only represents one version of the show. While the show is similar night to night, variation in phrase and detail between performances is a characteristic of the piece.*

Most of the text is delivered, conversationally, direct to the audience, as if sharing a story with friends. Music runs under much of the action, like a film score, stepping up in the physical sections.

OPENING

There is a chair downstage right, and upstage left in the back corner of the set. The table is against the back wall, underneath the cupboard doors.

As the audience enters, the WOMAN is practising shooting at a target, which hangs on the stage right door. The MAN sits on the chair downstage right. He ignores her and looks at the audience as they settle themselves.

THE GRASS IS GREENER

The MAN addresses the audience.

MAN: There's a saying, 'The Grass Is Greener'. The grass is greener in the next field it means, and it's true. The grass is greener on the other side of the fence. And tastier. And the cows in the next field are having a much better time than you are.

And the trouble is, there are plenty of holes in the fence, the farmer just doesn't maintain it properly, so it's very easy to slip through the fence and try out the new grass.

But then of course you realise that the new field is surrounded on all sides by other fields with really green grass in them… in fact, when you look, the green fields stretch out to the horizon like a patchwork quilt.

And at first, it's good fun, just running from one field to another to check out the different grass… but after a while it becomes this frantic quest to find the greenest grass…

And one day you stop and look back at the way you've come, at the fields you've been through. Some of them have had some good weather, and the grass is looking really green. And lush. And actually, when you think about it, it tasted pretty good, too, only you didn't stick around long enough to appreciate it.

And guess what? The farmer's been out and mended the fences, and put chains on the gates, and there's no going back.

The WOMAN approaches with gun and points it at the MAN, and addresses the audience.

WOMAN: You know sometimes he pisses me off so badly that I just want to blow his brains out. See them splatter against the back wall. See the blood slowly drip into his collar.

The WOMAN returns the gun and the target to the cupboard and closes the doors.

BEDROOM

The WOMAN takes a marker pen out of her pocket.

WOMAN: There's a room, and this is how I remember it.

She takes the cap off the pen and closes her eyes. She starts to draw on panel 1, drawing each object as she mentions it.

There are four walls. It's a bedroom.

Down this side of the room it's mainly windows. They're kind of old fifties style windows and open in odd ways and on this side of the room there's the door, built-in wardrobes – not very exciting, double bed. Very nice! Couple of pillows each and obviously a duvet. At this side...

MAN: Hang on, hang on, hang on. Have you got your eyes shut?

WOMAN: Yeah.

MAN: Okay.

WOMAN: At this side of the door there's a set of drawers and these are for things like knickers, socks, tights, that kind of thing. On top of that set of drawers there's another set of drawers only much smaller and in here there's kind of all different sorts of stuff.

There's some jewellery,

there's some hair slides in another,

I think in another one there's nail varnish,

in another one there's those little bottles that you buy when you're going on holiday and you don't want to take up much space in your wash bag and you fill it full of shampoo and stuff only no one can actually remember what's in the bottles because they've never labelled them so these kind of just build up with strange things in them.

Then there's one with kind of mediciney things in

and there's one with just kind of general rubbish in there, you know, things like rubber bands, tops off pens, old pairs of glasses that no one wears anymore. I think there's an old railcard in there that someone's kept because they like the photograph. That kind of thing – that lives in there.

And on top of the bigger set of drawers there's usually about three glasses of water and these are usually a few days old because someone's had it for drinking during the night and no one's laying claim to these glasses so they kind of just hang out there until they actually make it back to the kitchen.

On the other side of the door there's a chest. Don't know what's in it, it's not been unpacked since they moved in. And on top of there, there's a... there's a cheese plant on top of there. It's fairly healthy, just got a few brown bits round the edges. There's a waste paper basket there.

There's a laundry basket and usually the lid never shuts on this because it's absolutely packed with laundry coming out of the top.

Next to that there's a paper carrier bag. That's actually full of other nice carrier bags and then there's a table. Now various things land on this table depending on what day it is. On this particular occasion I think there's some receipts that someone's left. I think there might be a pair of tights that were on the floor and they've just been dumped there, and there's an old case full of make-up and there's things like some cheap hair lacquer in there and there's some fake tan and some moisturiser. That lives there.

At this side of the bed there's a bedside table and there's the usual sort of thing that you'd find on here so there's a kind of little lamp, paper shade, I think it came from Ikea, there's a clock, the alarm of which is always set about an hour later than the one on this side.

There's also a couple of books on the second shelf because this has shelves rather than drawers and on the bottom shelf there's a pack of condoms. In fact a pack of eighteen condoms because they buy them on their monthly shop to the supermarket so there's no argument over who buys what. This is her side of the bed.

Now on the other side of the bed there's not actually that much room between the bed and the wall and so stuff is kind of crammed down the side of it. I'm not really sure. I think there's definitely an alarm clock. It's one of those really annoying bell-type, old fashioned alarm clocks that ticks really loudly when you're trying to get to sleep.

She pauses.

MAN: Some books.

WOMAN: Some books? There's a couple of books stacked on top of each other but what I do know is these usually have sort of makeshift bookmarks made out of toilet paper in them and they kind of live there.

MAN: Magazines.

WOMAN: Magazines yes. There's a couple of magazines, which is an odd array. I think there's, on the bottom, I think there's a couple of cycling magazines and I think there's a copy of *Wired* there as well. I think... Is that about it?

MAN: Toilet roll.

WOMAN: Toilet roll, yes, toilet roll.

MAN: And there's a lamp.

WOMAN: Okay, so they're kind of down that side of the bed and then usually hanging around this area there's a pair of boxer shorts and a pair of knickers and usually, maybe the odd sock and they're trying to make their way into kind of this area.

She opens her eyes and looks at her drawing.

Yeah.

The WOMAN addresses the audience.

Basically it's a Sunday morning and there's two people and they're in bed and they're feeling absolutely terrible, they've been out on the piss the night before and they turn to each other and their breath smells, and they smile, and he ruffles her hair and she gently kisses him on the nose and then completely out of the blue he offers to go to the supermarket. Well she can't believe her luck but she's quite enjoying him being there so she tries to persuade him not to go but he's really adamant. He says that she can have whatever she wants, she can have croissants, she can have French bread, she can have fruit juice, she can have bagels, she can have fresh coffee, she can have fresh cereal, pretty much anything that's in the shop.

Well she tries to tell him to stay but he says no way and off he troops to the local supermarket and he comes back about half an hour later and he's got the Sunday papers, he's got loads of bags with him and you know she can hardly...

The MAN is laughing.

WOMAN: What is the matter with you?

MAN: Nothing

WOMAN: Nothing?

MAN: Carry on.

WOMAN: No, what?

MAN: Oh nothing. No sorry. The stuff about, OK. He went to the supermarket and he came back with some really nice stuff and they had a really nice breakfast, that's true. But it wasn't his idea to go to the supermarket and get all that stuff.

WOMAN: Yes it was.

MAN: No it wasn't

WOMAN: It was!

MAN: It wasn't his idea to go, it was her idea to go.

WOMAN: It was her idea to go?

MAN: Yes, she thought of it.

WOMAN: So you're calling me a liar?

ARGUMENT

An improvised argument ensues between the performers, about him undermining her in public and the nature of the relationship. It is short and becomes very heated. It ends with the WOMAN saying:

WOMAN: Ok there's two people and they're in bed and they turn to each other and they absolutely fucking stink because they've been out on the piss the night before and she kicks his lardy arse out of bed and he goes down the local shops and he buys half a dozen eggs, a few streaks of bacon and they have a fucking fry up!

The WOMAN storms to the back and sits. There is a moment's silence.

WOMAN: And it's really nice.

MOVING HOUSE

The MAN looks to the audience, then takes out his pen.

MAN: Okay. Okay.

He closes his eyes and starts to draw on panel 6 (back wall). It's a sitting room.

MAN: There's a room. It's quite a large room, there's a bay window down this side and the door's over here. It's lit by a bare light bulb. At the moment it's empty – well it's not really empty it's just that everything in it is all in boxes. There are stacks of boxes, cardboard boxes all along this wall, about three stacks I suppose. Each stack is about four or five boxes high. The boxes are all different sizes, they've been scrounged basically from various shops and they're full of books mainly, square things, I think there's one that's full of videos, maybe one of CDs but it's books mainly.

Also in the room there are lots of big, black bin bags. And these are full of squashy things, bedclothes, duvets, pillows, sheets, towels, dressing gowns, curtains, all the clothes that don't need hanging up, jumpers, pants, his trousers.

The clothes that do need hanging up are there as well, they're on the sofa.

There's a sofa but it's not like you could sit on it, it's on its end sticking up into the air and all the clothes are on hangers hanging down off it.

There's a table there too...

The WOMAN cross the stage and places the spare chair upside-down on the table.

... quite a large table and on top of it is another smaller table, a round table and this table's upside-down with its legs sticking up into the air. And nestled in between the legs of this small table are another couple of soft squashy bin bags and nestled in on top of them is a large, black video tape recorder. Also on top of the larger table there are a couple of plants.

There's a basil plant, quite a large bushy one but at the moment it needs watering a bit and there's a spider plant and that seems to be doing very well.

The WOMAN picks up the chair she is sitting on and places it upside-down on the table next to the first. She leans against panel 2.

There's another smallish table over here by the window and on top of that there are a couple of chairs and these too have been turned upside-down and they've also got their legs sticking up into the air.

There are some more boxes as well along this wall but these are different, they're shallow, they're almost like trays really, the kind of boxes that peaches come in at the market but with the blue plastic thing taken out. Anyway these boxes are full of kitchenware, saucepans, a frying pan, there's a really nice wok there that's been oiled and put into a plastic bag. There's also a lovely big, heavy, French cast-iron casserole dish and that's there too.

The MAN opens his eyes, views his work and writes 'MOVING HOUSE' under the image.

FURNITURE MOVING

The MAN and the WOMAN move the table to the centre of the room.

They move the table and chairs into different configurations, each one representing the layout of a past event. Each time the furniture is in place, they label the memories by writing phrases around the walls:

> DINNER PARTY WITH FRIENDS
>
> BURGLED – EVERYTHING GONE
>
> SUMMER – NEVER THERE
>
> THAT PATCH OF SUNLIGHT
>
> BONDAGE – FIRST TIME
>
> TELLING SOMEONE YOU CAN'T LIVE ANOTHER DAY WITHOUT THEM
>
> EXPENSIVE TAKEAWAY

The MAN and WOMAN move the table downstage centre. The MAN moves one chair in front of this, facing the audience, and sits.

> WORLD FAMOUS MIND READING GAMES

PILLS

The WOMAN sits on the chair up stage right. Throughout the MAN's monologue the WOMAN draws pill bottles on panel 7.

The MAN addresses the audience.

MAN: I'll tell you what works for me and that's drugs. Yes I'm afraid so. You see, drugs work. You can forget all about your Feng Shui. Your Tai Chi. Your Ch'i Kung. Your Yoga. Your vegetarian cycling holidays. Your walks in the country. Your family Christmases. That conversation you think you really ought to have with your parents. Those dreams you might have of maybe one day getting married and having kids. Finding that special person to grow old with.

It's not necessarily that those things are crap or that they're not worth having because I think they probably are. It's just that they're unreliable. They go wrong. Drugs, on the other hand, deliver the goods every single time. People say to me, you know they say 'Don't you think it's really sad that you need drugs to have a good time?' And I say 'No. It's excellent.' Because all I need is a reliable dealer and a ready supply of cash and I'm fine. I'm sorted.

I've got some drugs here, actually. Some of my favourite ones that you might be interested in.

The MAN gets up, takes his chair behind the table, and sits. He produces pill bottles from the table draw one by one as he describes each drug.

This one is a **Genuine Reaction Pill**. It's for those times when say you've got to meet someone at the station. A relative or an old friend and for whatever reason, I don't know, maybe you're tired, you can't be bothered or maybe you just don't like them, whatever. But it doesn't matter now because what I do is I take one of these pills and I will be completely over the moon when I catch sight of them and they will be so pleased to see how much I care.

This one is a **Perfect Excuse Pill**. I don't know about you, but I'm often late for things. I go into a room and there are all these expectant faces looking at me, they want to know why I'm late. And usually it's because, well I suppose it's because I can't be bothered to get there on time. But of course you can't say that so what I do is I take one of these. And then I come out with a really plausible, entertaining and authentic sounding excuse which everyone believes and which might even win me a bit of sympathy as well. Great.

This one is an **Easy Conscience Pill**. When you go out or even when you're in your own home there are adverts. People wanting your money. Good causes, charities and stuff but if you gave your money to all these people then you'd be skint within minutes. So what I do is I take one of these pills and then I can walk right past all the beggars on the street and still get that lovely warm, generous feeling as if I'd just given them fifty quid. And it won't have cost me a penny. Cool.

This one is an **I Look Great This Morning Pill**. Now I don't know about you but every morning I look and feel like absolute shit. So what I do is, before I look in the mirror, I take one of these pills and I look great! Well I don't really look any better but to me it'll seem like I do and that gives me the confidence to go out and face the day. Which is what it's all about.

This one is a **Not My Problem Pill**. Now a lot of things which make life more tolerable in this day and age, there's always some reason why you can't do them. For instance, fast food. It's cheap, it's tasty, it's convenient, but it's bad for the environment or the people who work there don't get paid properly or the animals get killed or something, I don't know. Your favourite brand of trainers: turns out they've been made by slaves. The bank with the most conveniently located cash machines manufactures land mines on the side or something. I mean you don't want to know about all that kind of stuff and neither do I so I take this pill and I realise that it is, of course, Not My Problem.

This one is a **Fall In Love With Someone Who's In Love With You Pill**. Now it doesn't happen to me very often but whenever someone does fall in love with me they're usually, well a right ugly fucker basically, they're following me around, I really can't be doing with it at all. So what I now do is I take one of these pills. And then I can shag them and have really good sex because we're both so in love and in the morning it's worn off so I can go on my way and everyone's happy. Some of these pills are actually quite strong and last a long time so use with caution.

This one is a **Final Word Pill**. It's for those times when you're having an argument with someone and they're winning, they're walking all over you and it's not until you've already stormed off and you're on the bus home that you think of that killer put down that you should have said. Well that doesn't happen to me anymore because what I do is, whenever there's an argument brewing I take one of these pills and come out with the perfect, witty, intelligent argument that makes whoever I'm arguing with look totally stupid. With this pill you are no longer afraid of public rows, I can tell you.

This one is a **Bar Presence Pill**. It's for when you're out on a Friday night and the place is full of weekend drinkers. Wankers who are nowhere to be seen during the week but are now there crowding the place and getting in the way and you can't even get served. Just take one of these pills and then you will immediately attract the bartender's attention.

The WOMAN opens the cupboard slowly takes out a knife, and approaches the man. She grabs him under the chin and holds the knife close to his throat. She addresses the audience.

WOMAN: Don't you think it's funny how the little things about someone that you totally fall in love with turn out to be the little things that really annoy you?

She talks to the MAN.

You're so funny aren't you! Absolutely hilarious! Is this funny?

She stabs knife into the table.

Ooops.

The WOMAN puts the pills back in the draw and slams it shut. She returns the knife to the cupboard.

GETTING TOGETHER

The MAN takes out his marker pen and draws on panel 9.

MAN: There's a room. It's kind of a kitchen/dining room. The door's over here. The kitchen bit of it is separated from the dining bit by a breakfast bar, which goes out into the middle of the room. This is the dining room bit and this is the kitchen bit. There's a cooker here, a gas cooker, and here's the sink and at the moment it's full of washing up, a couple of saucepans and I think there's a frying pan in there as well.

Just above the sink is a window. Now it's quite an old building and the walls are quite thick so there's a deep windowsill above the sink and there are a couple of things on it, there's a jam jar with some green water in it and out of the top of it there's some fresh coriander. Next to that there's a vase and it's one of those stupid vases that, even though it's quite big, can only hold one flower because the neck of it is so thin. And that's there too, empty of course.

Next to the sink there's a surface and on that is some more washing up, a stack of dirty plates with knives and forks on the top one along with a few little left-overs. I think there's also a colander there as well. Next to that is another surface but you can't really use that because immediately above it, mounted onto the wall is a gas boiler. It's one of those combination boilers that does the water as well as the heating so when you turn the water on it goes whoofghghghgh...

Next to that there's a door, which leads nowhere much. This is a basement flat so the door leads onto a basement area where there's a wall and on top of that is a flowerbed, which slopes up and away from the house. So if you're washing up at the sink and looking out of the window you get to see the flower bed from underneath, which is nice when the sun's shining because it shines through the green leaves of the flowers. There's also a tree out there, too, a large beech tree.

Anyway, next to the door is a fridge, it's a fridge/freezer which is quite tall, about this tall and on top of that is a portable CD, tape recorder thing and a little pile of CDs. Most of the CDs are with the main stereo in the other room but people have brought CDs into the kitchen to listen to while cooking or eating or whatever so all the popular CDs are here on top of the fridge. And most of them have got broken cases because they've fallen off onto the floor. It's a hard floor, a tiled floor, so anything you drop in here smashes.

Over here is the dining room bit. There's a large table and on either side of it there are wooden benches and there's a chair over at the end. On the breakfast bar there are more dirty plates, serving plates, a few empty wine bottles and an empty salad bowl with a bit of dressing in the bottom. Balsamic vinegar and olive oil.

On the table are a couple of bottles of wine, both of them about half full. There are also a few bowls, empty bowls with maybe a bit of rhubarb crumble in the bottom and they've all got spoons in. There's some glasses, wine glasses. Some of them are posh gobletty ones and some of them are just tumblers – a bit of a motley crew of glasses, mostly empty.

There's a fruit bowl full of, er, fruit: bananas, tangerines. Someone's got a tangerine and peeled it carefully, eaten the fruit and reconstructed it using the peel and that's on the table too and it's being used as an ashtray.

There's an empty chocolate box and there are little bits of foil everywhere, the chocolates were posh and came individually wrapped in foil and these wrappers have all been scrunched up into little balls. Someone has got theirs and meticulously flattened it out into a little square. Someone's even made theirs into a little figure and that's there too.

And there are hundreds of these tea lights everywhere, there's no lights on so all the light comes from these tea lights, there are hundreds of them. Well ten, maybe fifteen.

The MAN opens his eyes and looks at the drawing. He addresses the audience.

It's quite late, about midnight, one o'clock and there's been a dinner party. There's been about seven or eight people round the table and they're starting to go now. Three people go, they live on the other side of town and share a cab. Next there's a couple, they're on bikes, they go. Leaving three people round the table.

Now those three people are a man – he lives here, it's his flat – and two women. Now the women are a work colleague of the man and her flatmate. He knows the work colleague quite well, they've worked together for about two or three years and they're pretty good friends. He's met her flatmate twice maybe three times before and whenever they've met they've got on really well, they've talked for ages and when he invited his work colleague to the dinner party he said, 'Why don't you bring your flatmate along?' And she said then, she actually said, 'Do you fancy her?' And he said, 'No, no, not at all. I just want someone to make up the numbers.'

But during the evening they've been looking at each other, the man and the work colleague's flatmate, just a little bit whenever the man's said something particularly funny or amusing he's looked over at her to check out her reaction and she's always been laughing and tossing her hair a bit and they've caught each other's eye a few times. But the work colleague doesn't seem to have picked up on any of this, and she's still here. And she's beginning to talk about going home and shall they call a cab. And whenever she mentions this her flatmate doesn't agree or disagree she just ignores her basically and looks at the floor. So the man goes to the toilet. He doesn't really need to go but he wants to give the women the chance to work out a plan. While he's in the toilet he can hear them whispering and sure enough when he comes back into the kitchen his work colleague announces that she's going home and can he call a taxi for her. Which he immediately does.

Then they talk a bit the three of them. It's quite awkward though. Mercifully the cab arrives quite quickly though and there's a ring at the door. The work colleague gets up and moves towards the kitchen door. But before she leaves she asks her flatmate if she's going to be 'all right?' Her flat–mate doesn't say anything she just looks at the floor and nods. The man sees her work colleague out, he takes her to the front door, opens it for her. She kisses him on the cheek. Again it's quite awkward there. But anyway off she goes up the steps and into the waiting taxi. He closes the front door and locks it. Then he waits a moment before turning down the corridor and back into the kitchen.

The work colleague's flatmate is there sitting at the table and he goes to sit opposite her. They don't talk for ages they just look at the floor. Every now and then they look up, catch each other's eye and then immediately look away again, giggling. Not very mature behaviour for adults, but there you go.

The performers start to embody the story being told – not fully acting it out, but looking a bit coy at first, and then demonstrating the movements they describe.

They start to talk eventually though, what is it they talk about? Oh yeah, childhood. They share some family reminiscences, they talk about where they had holidays as kids and all that kind of stuff.

By now they are seated opposite each other at the table, centre stage.

WOMAN: Horoscopes.

MAN: Horoscopes yeah! They talk about horoscopes. It turns out that one of their descendants, ascendants or something are kind of fiercely opposed.

WOMAN: No it turns out…

MAN: … what?

WOMAN: … that he completely makes up a load of crap about
            horoscopes in an attempt to impress her but she knows
            more than he does.

MAN: And then she says she's got like a grandmother, basically
            a great aunt or a grandmother or something who's
            a gypsy, who's this gypsy, grandmother person who
            knows all about palmistry.

WOMAN: It's true! I do know all this stuff about palmistry

MAN: So she now starts to read his palm.

The WOMAN takes the MAN's hand as if starting to read his palm.

WOMAN: It's true because that there, that is your life line, that is
            your heart line…

MAN: … she doesn't know what she's talking about…

WOMAN: It's true! That is your heart line. And this line says that
            you are going to meet a small, very attractive dark-
            haired woman…

MAN: So she does all this stuff about palmistry… but earlier in
            the conversation he'd mentioned that he'd been to India…

WOMAN: Just the once? He mentioned it about five times that
            he'd been to India and while he was there he had in fact
            learnt this Indian head massage and he was like one of
            the few people in the country who could actually do this.

MAN: It's true yeah okay – only now is the time when she
            starts to get this pain in the neck and she mentions
            the pain in the neck about three or four times, and
            then finally he cottons on what he's supposed to do
            and he offers then to massage her so he massages her,
            massages her head and the cranium and then he starts

to do the small of her back because often if you've got problems in the neck the cause of it is further down. So he starts to massage her back and...

WOMAN: Yeah and he's tutting all the time, he's like doing this massage and he's just tutting really loudly until he finally confesses that he can't actually deliver this massage to its full effect while she's still wearing clothes.

MAN: It's true! He hardly even finishes this sentence before she whips off her jersey and puts it on the floor and she's there in her bra wanting to be massaged, yeah, so he obviously continues to massage her next to her skin and he's really sort of getting in there and suddenly without a word of explanation she leaps up out of her chair and gets on the table so obviously he can't massage her any more.

The WOMAN sits on the table in front of the MAN. They are very close.

WOMAN: And she sits on the table, edges over and leans back casually and knocks a bowl of rhubarb and custard onto the floor and it literally smashes, all over.

MAN: It's not one of the expensive bowls so it's not a problem, but he gets up and kind of looks where it is and sort of leaning over her shoulder looking down kind of saying, ooh, erm...

WOMAN: For quite a long time...

MAN: Yeah...

WOMAN: ... as I remember.

They stay close to each other as they explain what follows, but don't actually kiss or undress.

MAN: Then he turns to face her and her face is like right there, erm... and they start snogging.

WOMAN: Yeah. It's very nice.

MAN: Yeah.

          He's got his hand on her knee as well, she's wearing a
          skirt and his hand's on her knee. Then he starts to kiss
          her neck I think.

WOMAN: Yeah and her hands are trying to lightly brush the back
          of his neck and kind of tickle down the sides of his body.

MAN: And he starts to kiss her shoulder and he comes across
          her bra strap so he kind of pulls it to one side...

WOMAN: Yeah.

MAN: And she does this funny thing with her arm, getting
          her hand out of the bra and the bra strap's just hanging
          there and I think with a bit of help the bra basically
          exposes one of her breasts and he starts to kiss it, starts
          to kiss her nipple.

WOMAN: And he's kind of leaning in to her quite a lot at this point
          so she can obviously feel that he's got, you know, a hard-
          on, so she decides that she's kind of, moves things on
          a bit and then works her hand round to the front and
          to his belt and she kind of fumbles, fumbles about a bit
          with this belt.

MAN: She's spending ages trying to undo his belt and she can't
          do it.

WOMAN: Hoping he's not noticing.

MAN: But he lets her kind of fumble away for a bit and then,
          I don't think he says anything, he just starts to do it
          himself and takes it...

WOMAN: He just does it.

MAN: ... off completely and I think while he's about it he does or undoes his trousers and his flies and his trousers...

WOMAN: ... fall down...

MAN: Yeah.

WOMAN: With a bit of help maybe.

MAN: ... down to his ankles and then he starts like, they start snogging again, even more and his hands starts working their way up her leg and reaches the top of her leg and he discovers at that point that she's not wearing any knickers.

WOMAN: He's pleasantly surprised that she's not wearing knickers.

MAN: Yeah, yeah, pleasantly surprised, yeah, pleasantly surprised. And he feels that she's quite wet so I think at that point he realises where this situation's leading so he's got some condoms in the bedroom so he sort of goes over to the door...

WOMAN: Waddles.

MAN: Yeah, he's got his trousers round his ankles so he's kind of waddling and she tries to follow him but he says 'no, no', I don't think he says anything, rather he just kind of motions for her to stay on the table and he goes over out the kitchen and into the bedroom and he takes off his shoes and his trousers and I think his pants and puts on a condom and then he comes back into the kitchen with his condom on.

WOMAN: And his socks.

MAN: It's a cold floor, there's tiles, it's a cold floor. He comes in and then she's...

WOMAN: Oh she's, yeah, she's kind of leaning back at this point trying to look really seductive. She's got herself sorted you know, and taken off her bra and things.

MAN: She's got her skirt kind of up like that, sticking her tits out. And he, well he sticks his cock in –

WOMAN: They fuck on the table.

MAN: Then he sort of carries her, still inside her, into the bedroom and then they just collapse on the bed.

WOMAN: I think they talk for a bit.

MAN: Yeah, they talk and after a while they stop talking and they get really drowsy and he gets out of bed and turns off the light and they both get under the covers and they fall asleep.

A pause.

RUNNING

The WOMAN moves and sits on a chair and addresses the audience.

WOMAN: Everyone around me seems to have taken up running. They run as often and as fast as they possibly can and they develop asthma, bulimia, manic depression and they smoke too many fags, drink too much booze, work ridiculous hours for careers that they really feel are worth it. They exercise body and mind at any free opportunity. They go to Goa to discover themselves and they meditate and they detox and they just keep on running.

And they are, on the whole, sensible, logical people. They say they've no need of a therapist, they've no need of a priest, and they are right. Because as long as they keep on going they're okay, you see, it's when you stop you have problems. It's when you stop you start to think and if you start to think then you start to assess and if you start to assess then you have to ask questions and ultimately you have to come up with answers and being a cynical bastard in the first place you probably won't like the answers that you come up with and so you'll have to make changes which let's face it would be far too scary a thought.

I have done lots of things to try and make myself happy. I've done selfless deeds and gestures for other people. I've tried blending in. I tried sitting for a really long time on my own trying to work out what it is I want. Tried re-arranging the furniture. Tried re-inventing myself. I even tried not watching the news but none of it actually seems to work.

So I bought myself a pair of trainers, I'm going to take up jogging and pretty soon I reckon I can be running as often and as fast as all the rest of them.

INDIA

A clock ticks. The WOMAN puts her chair underneath the table and walks to the back wall. She closes her eyes and begins to draw on panel 4.

WOMAN: There's a room and it's an L-shaped room and there's not really that much in it. There's a little tiny window here but it's very high up and it's very small and it's absolutely filthy so it doesn't really do its job at all. In the room, well, there's a wooden table and this is an old kind of rickety wooden table where people have etched their initials onto the top. There's something like DM 4 ZW or something like that, just scratched in the top of the table and then there's a couple of, kind of dining room style chairs but one of them is not very good because you actually have to lean it against the wall if you want to sit on it because it's only got three legs.

On top of the table there's a bowl and this is a white ceramic bowl, with one of those with blue edging just around the top and in a similar style next to it there's a jug and that contains yesterday's water, because this is meant for washing but it's a little bit rusty so you wouldn't really want to use it.

On the other side of the room there's the bed, obviously, a double bed, very uncomfortable, springs coming through, makes lots of noise when you try to turn over. There's a couple of pillows, the feathers come out during the night, tickling your nose and there's a single sheet, only that's got some brown stains in the corner. I'm not really sure what they are.

There's a couple of rucksacks in there, they've been travelling and have seen better days, stuff is coming out of the top of them and there's also some shopping from the local market, they've been and done some shopping. There's some local bread, there's a couple of oranges and I think there's definitely a bottle of mineral water.

The WOMAN opens her eyes and addresses the audience.

And this is a hotel room in India and it's a bit run down. They could afford better hotels, better rooms at the start of their holiday but they've run out of money and they don't get very much sleep because the neighbours are very noisy, shouting at each other while they're trying to get some sleep.

And it's very humid, the fan in their room has in fact broken and so there's no fresh air coming in. It's very stale and very smoky and the cockroaches scuttle out from underneath the bed at night just as you put your head on the pillow. He seems to pace the room continuously. They don't really talk to each other very much.

Movement sequence: time passing. The performers shift positions in the room. There is a constant sense of them almost touching, almost communicating, the WOMAN attempting to touch or connect with the MAN, and him always (unintentionally?) moving away at the last minute.

They end up sat on the table next to each other, facing the audience.

WOMAN: Why didn't you tell me if you didn't want to be with me?

The MAN stands and moves behind the table.

MAN: Because I didn't want to be on my own.

WOMAN: Right. That's nice. You stayed with me because you didn't want to be on your own.

The MAN goes to the cupboard and takes out the rope, then holds the rope around the WOMAN's throat. As he speaks he does a rope trick, so it appears to pass through the WOMAN's neck.

MAN: You know sometimes she just talks and talks and talks and that's all she does, she just talks, you know, and she's always right. You know sometimes I just want to shut her up, I just want to stop those words in her throat.

As the MAN returns the rope to the cupboard, the woman exits stage left.

WOMAN: Well. Guess what. You can be on your own.

The WOMAN exits through the door stage left.

MONOPOLY

MAN: Okay. Fine.

He moves to the table.

    There's a game. It's quite a common game, I'm sure most of you have played it before.

He takes a Monopoly set out of the table draw. During the following speech he sets out the board and the pieces for the start of a game.

It's called Monopoly. It's a board game and the aim of the game is to acquire wealth through property.

There's a board, fake money, each of you chooses a funny little thing to be, there's a car, an ocean-going liner, a boot and an iron. I don't know what an iron's got to do with it all but there you go. There are various cards that you have to pick up if you land on certain squares, these are called Chance cards and these are called Community Chest for some reason. They're just like the Chance cards really except that they're pink.

Anyway you go round the board, rolling the dice, and if you land on a property square then you can buy it, provided of course that no one has bought it already. You can't do that anyway on the first circuit because you can't buy anything until you've been round the board once. If you do buy a property then you get a little card to prove it, and if people land on your property they have to pay you rent. At this stage of the game that's not a big problem though, because rents are quite low. This one, for example. Leicester Square, twenty-six quid.

As the game progresses, though, it gets more difficult because what people do is they begin to acquire monopolies. What that means is that they've somehow managed to buy a complete set, say all the greens or all the yellows. That's called a monopoly and when you've got a monopoly then you can start to build on your properties, houses and hotels. And that affects the rents. For example Leicester Square with four houses and a hotel is six hundred pounds.

Now at this stage of the game, when there are houses and hotels around, having to pay those kinds of rents can bankrupt people so to stay in the game people do a lot of off the board dealing, they're borrowing money off each other, they're selling each other properties, all sorts of stuff like that goes on and that's perfectly legal.

The WOMAN enters stage right.

It's part of the game. Now some games can go on for a long time. I've known games to last four or five hours and people want to stop. They've got to go, they're losing or they're just plain bored, that can happen. And that's allowed, that's fine, in fact it says in the rules what happens, what should happen, when someone wants to leave the game.

The MAN moves away from the table and reads from the instructions. Whilst he's doing this the woman stands by the table and quietly makes some adjustments to the money different players have got.

MAN: Should a player for any reason wish to retire from the game before he or she has been made bankrupt, one of two things may happen.

1) They can give all their money and properties to the bank, the properties then being put up for sale in the usual way

or 2) they can simply withdraw their money and properties from the game altogether.

Now. Nowhere in the rules does it say that a player who wishes to retire from the game can just give all their properties and money to one other person, thereby completely upsetting the balance of the game and showing a lot of favouritism as to who they give their money and properties to...

WOMAN: Alright, there's a room –

She has her eyes closed and draws on panel 8.

and it hasn't got any windows because it's a kind of den. People go in there late at night. There's an open staircase that leads down into the room but the main thing that occupies this room is in fact a sofa. Now this sofa is really nice, a big three-seater sofa, I think it's probably from Habitat. You can sit on the arms. I mean this is the kind of sofa where you would lose friends down between the cushions for about a week and it's really nice so everyone's sort of piled on there at the moment.

At the side of that there is a bookshelf and you can find the usual suspects on here you know, there's a few Rough Guides, maybe a couple of graphic novels, maybe some cookery books and they're on there.

On top of the bookcase there's a CD player and that's been going for most of the evening. We've had things like David Gray, Massive Attack, bit of Portishead. At the side of that there's a rocket shaped lava lamp and that's got black ink in it going up and down and there's a plant between that and the settee and that's a weeping, some kind of weeping fig – that's there.

Now at the other side of the settee there is a waste paper basket and there's also a chair, an easy chair. Now it doesn't actually fit in style with this one, I think it's second hand but it's still very comfy and there's three people on here kind of playing musical chairs because each time the person who's got the comfy seat in the middle goes to the toilet the other people on the arms jump in and sit there.

At the side of that there's a dining room chair. It doesn't usually live in here. It's covered in fake cowhide. It is in fact a dining room table chair and it's been brought in especially for this occasion because there's extra friends round.

There's also a table and most of the games the household owns are kept on here and everything else has been cleared off due to the party and there's lots of bottles, empty bottles, bottles of lager.

And there's also a couple of very nice triangular shaped ashtrays, very stylish, but these are full of tab ends and fag butts and things like that.

And so the table is near the chair that's been shipped in and at the other side of the stairs there is in fact a beanbag, and this beanbag is just on the edge of the rug that dominates most of the room.

Someone is sat in this beanbag at the moment and it's pretty unusual because let's face it, people don't usually like to end up with the beanbag because you can't support your back and you have to keep getting in and out. But this person has actually sought out the bean bag and is sat in it and has pretty much managed to isolate themselves from the rest of the group from the moment they've arrived by choosing this seat.

The WOMAN opens her eyes.

Oh and there's also...

She draws the board with her eyes open.

... a game of Monopoly.

Now it's about, I don't know, half past eleven on a Friday evening and it's a group of friends and they've all come round and they've decided to have a cheap night in basically, instead of going to the pub so they've been having a laugh and they've been chatting and they've been drinking their beer and generally having a good time and then someone decides that they should get out the Monopoly. Well there's a few boos but most of the people in the end agree to go along with it. So they get out the Monopoly.

No one is going to take this game of Monopoly seriously at all apart from one person who...

The MAN starts drawing on panel 2.

MAN: There's a room, it's a very small room, small because it's really only supposed to be used by one person at a time. There's a toilet over here and above that is a cistern and above that is a little window and on the windowsill is a basket of dried flower petals that are supposed to smell nice but don't. On the door is a lock and a toilet-roll holder with some toilet roll in it.

He opens his eyes.

Now this small room that's really only supposed to be used by one person at a time is at the moment being used by two people. 'Why?' you might ask. Well there's a drug. It's a very expensive drug and one of the two people in the small room has got a bit. But she's too mean to share it out so she makes a secret little signal to her Special Friend and goes to the small room. After about ten seconds the Special Friend makes up some feeble excuse and disappears.

Now after about a quarter of an hour the partner of the woman with the drug begins to wonder where she's got to. So he goes and has a look round the flat. He goes to the kitchen and she's not there, he tries the bedroom and she's not there either so eventually he goes to the small room and he knocks at the door. There's no answer. So he tries to open the door. It's locked. So he says, he says 'Are you all right?' There's a silence. Then there's a little giggle. Then there's another little giggle, coming from a different mouth. So he goes back to the other room.

WOMAN: So everyone thinks that they've come round to have quite a good laugh and basically to enjoy themselves so they set off with this game of Monopoly and it's taken far too seriously by one of the members of the group. So much so that not only does he take his money but he also takes the dice to the toilet to stop people cheating. I mean get a life.

Now the girlfriend that he's with is actually very nice. You know, she's out for a laugh, she wants to talk to everyone. She's good friends with everybody and so when the person who owns this flat, who happens to be male comes over and asks if he could have a quiet word, she's more than happy to oblige. So they just go off to the... they just happen to be in the toilet because one of them needs a wee...

MAN: Alright! There's two people in the small room. They've been gone for about an hour...

WOMAN: They have not!

MAN: It's been about an hour...

WOMAN: It's not an hour!

MAN: After about half an hour it's getting ridiculous, the
          partner of the woman with the drug is trying to get on
          with the game but it's ground to a halt because it's the
          turn of one of the people in the small room and they're
          not here. Everyone knows where they are because
          someone's tried to use the small room for the purpose
          for which it was intended and can't because it's locked
          and everyone's looking at him, the partner of the woman
          with the drug who's now in the small room with her
          special friend and thinking, what must he be thinking,
          how must he be feeling but it's something that no one
          wants to ask and he's thinking, what must they be
          thinking about him just sitting there while all this is
          going on, and eventually he can't stand it anymore so he
          goes back to the – alright he walks quietly up to the – he
          creeps up to the door of the small room and he listens.
          And he hears... He's not quite sure what he hears but
          they're not talking. They're not talking in there.

The MAN sits in a chair upstage left corner.

WOMAN: I'll tell you what he hears – he hears little voices inside
          his head, that's what he hears because basically all
          they've done, as I say, this person wanted to have a chat,
          the guy has found out that the woman he's in love with
          is in love with somebody else. He's totally heartbroken,
          he's not stealing anybody else's girlfriend or boyfriend,
          they are just talking in the toilet – that's all they're
          doing and there's nothing wrong as far as I know with
          a woman and her very good friend, I would like to say,
          sharing a bit of quality time and just talking about
          things that's all they did.

The WOMAN draws two stick figures talking, on panel 8.

The MAN draws a stick figure blow job picture, on panel 3.

WOMAN: What hasn't been mentioned is that she came out of the toilet and she went home with the grumpy bastard and she shared a bed with the grumpy bastard because she happened to live with the grumpy bastard because at that point, whether it was foolish or not, she actually believed that she was in love with him.

And it's just a shame that he couldn't see it really.

The MAN leaves through the door, stage right.

I'M A LIAR

The WOMAN packs the game away and addresses the audience.

WOMAN: I'm a liar. I lie. I tell lies. I make things up, tell little fibs, rearrange the truth to suit myself and I'm economical with it. I lie and I'm not ashamed of it. I weave my web of deceit and I lasso my victims like a Rhinestone Cowboy. I lie.

I tell people, my friends, that they look nice when they don't. When people ask me if I'm OK I say 'yeah', when I feel like shit. I profess to fancying people when I know in my heart of hearts that I can't. And most of the time they're little white ones. It's only occasionally that they're great big black ones. I deceive people. I look them in the eye and lie to both them and myself. I'm a liar. I tell lies.

The MAN returns.

THE END

MAN: I've got another game.

WOMAN: Oh great.

MAN: Close your eyes.

WOMAN: Why?

MAN: Close your eyes

WOMAN: Okay. My eyes are closed.

The MAN takes the blindfold from the cupboard and blindfolds the WOMAN. During these next lines, he moves the table and a chair downstage left, facing diagonally into the room, takes the 'weapons' that haven't been used so far out of the cupboard and places them on the table. He briefly exits stage left and fetches the polythene sheeting from backstage, lays it in the middle of the room and places the other chair on it.

MAN: You know sometimes I think that I really want to leave her but the thought of her being alive and with someone else...

The MAN manoeuvres the blindfolded WOMAN onto the chair on the polythene, centre stage. The MAN sits down behind the table.

          Imagine for some reason you... had to leave the world. What would you miss?

A pause.

WOMAN: I'd miss...

          I'd miss really nice bunches of flowers that smell really lovely

          and I'd miss shouting

          I'd miss swearing

          and I'd miss the feeling that you get as though your heart's going to break in two and you can hardly breathe when the person that you love leaves you.

          And I'd miss spending too long waiting for the telephone to ring and I'd miss, I'd miss crap telly and vegging out like a couch potato.

I'd miss feeling stupid at, at crying, crying when friends or family do things I'm really proud of and weeping for no reason.

I'd miss, I'd miss the fact that I've never really done anything really exciting. Never had the opportunity.

I'd miss going into posh shops and trying on lots of outfits that I can't afford just to piss the shop assistants off.

I'd miss really nice spicy food that by the time you've finished the meal you feel that you can breathe fire.

I'd miss laughing. I'd miss being with a group of people and everyone is just really doing big belly laughs and it's like everyone just forgets who they are.

And I'd miss the tingly feeling that makes your hair stand on end the first time you touch somebody.

By the end of the WOMAN's 'I Would Miss' list, the MAN has returned all the weapons to the cupboard, closed it and written 'THE END' over the cupboard doors.

He joins the WOMAN, squeezing onto the chair with her, putting his arm around her.

During this speech the WOMAN removes her blindfold.

MAN: I'll miss drinking tea.

I'll miss drinking tea in the morning. I'll miss tea. I'll miss being brought a cup of tea in bed in the morning and the person who's brought it getting back into bed.

I'll miss cold days. I'll miss staying in on a cold Saturday afternoon watching rugby on the telly, the players all muddy while I sit there as it gets dark outside.

I'll miss welcoming someone in and feeling their cold nose on my cheek.

I'll miss afternoons in smoky pubs with a shaft of sunlight coming in.

I'll miss riding my bike.

I'll miss getting a minicab back from the pub, gliding past the gangs of drunks on the street, looking at the lights on the dashboard all green and yellow and red and miss the opportunity, just the opportunity, of telling the taxi driver to keep driving, to drive all night so I can watch the sun come up somewhere else.

The MAN takes his arm from around the WOMAN's shoulders.

They are left sharing the chair, alone.

The lights fade to black.

Poster and flyer images.

Rachael Walton in *Presumption* publicity shot.
Photo: Rob Hardy.

PRESUMPTION

Performance text by
Alexander Kelly
Chris Thorpe
Rachael Walton

Best Laid Plans

Presumption began in a company meeting, early in 2005. In the midst of discussing something else entirely, Rachael had a flash of inspiration. What if a show started with a woman backing onto a stage, carrying a tray, and talking to people offstage, 'in another room'? What if she turned round, still talking to the other people, to put the tray of glasses and crockery onto the table but the table is not there and so the tray falls to the floor and all the glasses break? She realises she does not have a set/any furniture, sees the audience, and is momentarily confused: where is all the stuff? What is expected of her? The confusion is partly between performer and character. And then she just gets on with it. She starts to build the set/bring the furniture on from the wings herself.

A few months later we tried this out. A twenty-five-minute work-in-progress performance that we called *Best Laid Plans*, as part of Sheffield Theatres' *Pyramid Project*. From that starting point, Rachael repeatedly disappeared offstage to get another piece of furniture, and heaved it onto the stage. An armchair. A desk. A heavy computer monitor. A massive rug. A couple of cushions thrown on from the wings. Whenever we improvised this, we really liked the moment when the random collection of objects, with the addition of just one more item, suddenly looked like a room. A room where people lived, where things had happened. We liked how we could drop in clues to stories. Bringing on an armful of games, Rachael removed a few jigsaw pieces and hid them in the armchair. Each time she positioned a piece of furniture, she checked its position by half-performing a fragment of text or action, narrating to herself: 'So I sit here, turn and look at him, there, and say, no, sorry, I don't agree.' Satisfied that the chair, for example, was in the right place, she would then head off for something else.

Performers do not usually go offstage in Third Angel shows. It was quite a big thing for us when the WOMAN and the MAN both go off in *Where From Here*. Because performers are (nearly) always themselves, or themselves as well as the character or persona they are presenting to the audience; they are always aware that they are sharing a space with the audience and spending time with them. So usually they stay on, and watch, even if they have nothing to 'do'. We talk about performers being on-off.[1] They are still onstage, but they are not asking for the audience's attention.

We had thought that Alex would also be in this early version, taking it in turns to drag something on, but in the week-long making process, we couldn't make it work with two people, so we kept it to just Rachael. When it is a solo performance, going offstage is even more challenging. We thought of *Best Laid Plans* partly as an experiment to see how long an audience would watch a bare stage if they were waiting for something to be brought on. We worked out that the stage was empty (of people) for about half the length of the piece.

Audience feedback was positive. People did not mind the waiting – enjoyed it even. They liked how difficult some of the heavier pieces of furniture were to bring on. They were intrigued by the fragments of story that the task of the show offered them. We realised we were on to something. We were not sure if we had the first half hour of a show, or a full-length piece condensed to 25 minutes. As is often the case, it turned out that what we had was something between the two.

---

1   A phrase we picked up from the way Forced Entertainment talk about this mode of performance.

A Show About Love

One of the things that we particularly liked about *Best Laid Plans* was the way Rachael performed it, with the energy of actors doing a line run after a few days off, or a mark-through on the stage without full performance volume or physicality; a private ritual in preparation for a performance.

Planning the development of a two-person show, initially we planned to write, or in fact commission, a whole new play, which we would then only ever see fragments of, out of order, instigated by the different pieces of furniture being positioned, like we had in *Best Laid Plans*. The audience would be invited to piece together the narrative as the fragments of story and items of furniture built up on the set. But that is a very odd gig to offer a writer and so after some discussion we moved on from that idea. We knew that the show was about a couple, and so we decided that we would devise a bank of material – conversations, domestic interactions, confessions – that we could then draw upon for the show.

We talked about the couple, sharing a flat after being together for seven years. We talked about not knowing whether you are in love or not, and not knowing how to find out, because so many of the love stories in films, and books and songs, are about the thrill of getting together or the heartbreak of splitting up. We had discovered that *Where From Here* was about love during the devising process. This time we decided in advance that the show was about love. Not an intense, when do we see each other next, new-romance love. Nor a saddened, embittered, heartbroken love, but the place in-between. A love that has grown over years to the point where getting on with life has taken over. Where it is no longer clear whether the feelings have become a deeper, more integral part of you, or whether the relationship has just become habit. We talked about couples stuck in a situation where they are pretending it is the former, because to question the sincerity of the emotion is too dangerous, as that would mean a complete life change.

We talked a lot about our own experiences and expectations. We talked about our parents and grandparents. About generations before us who were so busy working and supporting children they never had the luxury to wonder if they were happy together or not. We talked about people stuck in a relationship because they simply could not afford to separate, to leave their shared house or flat.

Parallel Tracks

Early 2006. We had recently begun developing a show about air-crash investigation[2] with Chris Thorpe, and we asked him if he would like to be part of what we were now calling *Presumption*. The process marked a shift in our practice, being the first one to allow for the fact that as a company we were starting to have children. Rachael was just back from maternity leave, and so we made the show part-time over about four months. This demanded more flexibility of the making team, but allowed more thinking and design time outside of the rehearsal room.

The devising process had two parallel strands: the relationship and the furniture. Unusually for a Third Angel process we were developing characters right from the outset, trying them on, fleshing out their relationship. We decided that the couple were called Beth and Tom, and we began having Rachael and Chris improvise long conversations between them, about issues or situations in their lives, which we would record and transcribe. We used other text-generating improvisations and writing exercises, too: describing their backstories, writing letters between them, inviting them to talk to the audience about what was going on. Our menu of material about their lives, and the central questions of the show, built up to be several hours of material. Like many devising processes, we log sections we're interested in – material that is 'in play' – on index cards, or post-it notes, or pieces of torn A4. These sections were all stored in columns taped to the wall, to remind us what we had got, and to enable us to experiment with different orders.

2   *Parts For Machines That Do Things*, which would
     eventually be shown in 2009.

Some of these sections were well developed. Some even had their own soundtracks. Composer David Mitchell was in the making room with us a lot, creating the soundtrack, even though we did not know yet how the show would actually work. Several of the speeches had music to accompany them, even though we did not know for definite that they would be in the show.

At the same time, we continued developing the task of bringing the furniture and props on in different ways, from overtly physical and theatrical to unassuming and entirely functional. We began to build up a menu of ways to bring the objects on, and attitudes to the task. We started to design and build some bespoke pieces of furniture, built by our friends at prop-makers Vision Works, so they were lighter and more manoeuvrable than real furniture. David had even given the furniture task its own soundtrack, too: a record player needle stuck in the run-out grooves of a vinyl LP.

As the weeks passed, and the opening date drew nearer we could not find an order for the material to work. We could not get the two strands to connect. One person struggling on with a living room's worth of stuff and occasionally hiding some jigsaw pieces under a sofa cushion had been good fun as a solo show. But, as we had instinctively known, as soon as you knew there was a second person in the wings, the immediate thought was 'Why aren't they helping?' The task of the show didn't make sense. We were also interested in making a show that tidied itself away. We were working with an idea that the show would get to the point where there would be loads of stuff onstage, that they were trapped by it all, but then gradually it would disappear again. Of course, this doubled the length of the task.

We still enjoyed the tone of the fragments of the text that the furniture positioning produced, but it did not allow for much variation or, indeed, for the sharing of much of the material we had generated. After a fairly depressing run one Friday afternoon, we looked at the huge list of sections up on the wall, and the rehearsal room full of furniture, and we knew it was not working.

What If It Works The Other Way Round?

With each project we are looking for the frame of the show; the rules, the task. What is the level of fiction? What is the performers' relationship with the audience? How is the story told? Once we have that mechanism, we are able to start ordering the material, start cutting stuff out and looking for gaps.

wine - 2nd glass - refers a bit more to the scene?
is drunk
wine bar - same wine?

DON'T NOT LOVE - more live run in middle + end
do these things again .

LATCH ON
CABINET - R
SOFA
COFFEE TABLE
MAGAZINES / POLAROID
CHAIRS '2 PEOPLE'
LAMP - R
BOOKSHELVES
SCREEN
BOOKS + ORNAMENTS
PHOTO
DESK
PHONE
WINE GLASSES
BOOZE - C
TABLE CHAIRS
DON'T NOT LOVE HER
DO THE MATHS
PEANUT

. . . .

DIRECT LOTHAR
BASK LOTHAR
TALK BOY
LOTHAR

RUNNING ORDER 28.4.06

2 MAY 2006.

A new idea from Rachael - actually more task based, but more 'real' response to the fictional dilemma that we originally set ourselves (or at least the performers).

They try to perform the show / play (in this version the distinction is blurred / chosen) but they only go to get the furniture required when they encounter it (or its absence).

This would make more sense at the start - but would it still allow us to go into the Wine Glasses stuff (for example?). I think so. In fact I think we would need to - to break out of the rules of this game.

It is a more co-operative brief... they have to work to 'fill' on their own perhaps! What we realised talking today was that the 2-hander is much less forgiving of dead space, and the simple furniture task... why don't they both do more?

QUESTIONS: What is the script order? Does this approach work? What existing material does it allow?

The following Monday morning Rachael came in and said, 'What if it works the other way round? What if, instead of each piece of furniture prompting a little bit of text, they try to play out a scene, have a conversation, and each time they need to sit somewhere, or use something, they have to stop and go and get it? And then start again?'

And in that thought, we had the show. We understood the mechanism by which the two strands could interact, and by lunchtime we had the first half of the show assembled.

From the list of long conversations that Chris and Rachael had improvised, we chose the one we called 'Infidelity', which took place after a dinner party, after the guests had all gone home. We knew then that we didn't need any of the other conversations we had logged – this would be the one they would keep trying to have. We realised that the 'line-run' energy that we liked so much was the way in to the restarts and repeats, and that it needed to develop into the same text being played with very different attitudes. We were aware, too, of course, that this repetition of the text also stood in for the daily grind of their relationship being played out each day. Building around this, we understood which asides and audience-aware sections were required, and we knew what needed to be different in the second half, as the narrative moves into the next day, and becomes concerned with the future.

Happy Accidents

This new structural idea meant that we had to have a clear room layout. We laid out the furniture in a definitive pattern. We marked the positions on the floor. We cleared the furniture away. The empty floor markings were great. Like an architect's drawing and a crime scene. We decided to keep them, to make them more visible, in fact. At about this time lighting designer Jim Harrison realised that the key to the show was not to light the performers directly, but instead to light each piece of furniture as it came on, so that more of the stage came alive as the show progressed.

Several of our shows before *Presumption* had been about time,[3] and this was a theme we were still interested in. But we knew we wanted the piece to think about the future. If Beth and Tom did stick together, until they were old, what would it be like? We had an improvisation game

3   *Realtime* (2004), *Hurrysickness* (2004), as well as *Standing Alone, Standing Together* (2005) to some extent.

that predicted events in their future, but it felt too listy to use much of it.[4] At some point Alex was out in a hire van mid-afternoon, collecting furniture. The van radio was tuned to Radio 2, and he just left it on. Steve Wright and his team were sharing factoids. One of them was that over the course of your lifetime, you will spend 38 days looking for things in the fridge. It sounded ludicrous. But when we did the maths, we realised it was possible. It gave us the peg we needed to hang the discussion of the future on.

Touring

We opened *Presumption* in May 2006, with a week's run in the Crucible Studio in Sheffield, performed by Rachael and Chris. The following year, Rachael redirected the show with Lucy Ellinson in her role. Usually after a show has opened we will rework sections, sometimes quite substantially, in response to what we have learned about it through sharing it with audiences. With *Presumption* it was just a case of fine-tuning, tightening up, polishing the text, making a couple of sections more personal to Lucy's version of Beth. This version of the show opened at Birmingham Rep in February 2007, and toured throughout the UK, to the Intercity Festival in Florence, before a week at the Edinburgh Fringe as part of the British Council Showcase in August 2007. This in turn led to more international bookings, and over the following 18 months *Presumption* became our most performed show with gigs in Brussels, Barcelona, Clonmell, Moscow, Yerevan, Mannheim and Lisbon, before returning for runs in London, Leicester and a great one-off show at ARC in Stockton.

We never actually retired *Presumption*, but other projects and opportunities took over, and the show ended up taking a six-year break. In October 2015, we remounted the touring version of *Presumption*, with Lucy and Chris, in Sheffield, to mark our 20th Anniversary as a company.

---

4   You can hear the remnants of this When We Are Older game when they talk about their cottage in the country towards the end of the play.

The following year we returned to the original pairing of Rachael and Chris, for performances at Northern Stage in Newcastle. Around this time, Lucy remarked that usually, when you stop doing a show after a long run, it is like taking a piece of furniture out of your living room. You miss it at first, but gradually the indentations in the carpet fade. With *Presumption*, she said, the indentations have never completely gone. And when it came to rehearsal, we all found that the show was buried not too deeply in our memories.

Third Angel presents
PRESUMPTION

Devised and Written by
Alexander Kelly, Chris Thorpe & Rachael Walton

Performed by
Rachael Walton (2006 & 2016)
Lucy Ellinson (2007–2015)
Chris Thorpe

Directed and Designed by
Rachael Walton & Alexander Kelly

Lighting Design
James Harrison

Music and Sound Design
David Mitchell

Technical Manager & Re-light
Martin Fuller

Touring Stage Manager
Helen Fagelman

Set Construction
Vision Works

Management
Hilary Foster
Tracey Doxey

With thanks to:
Paul Fraser; Julie Horan; Stella McCabe; Angela Galvin, Ellie Jones and everyone at Sheffield Theatres; Dead Earnest Theatre; Unlimited Theatre; Alison Andrews, Mark Hollander, David Micklem; Annie Lloyd; Gordon Scott; John Green; Steve Curtis; Rachael Spence; Cassie Friend; Rosi Hunter; Patti Doxey; Barry Ryan; all of our partner venues on the 2007 tour.

Presumption was first presented at the Crucible Theatre Studio, Sheffield, 17 May 2006, performed by Rachael Walton and Chris Thorpe. It was restaged in 2007, with Rachael directing and Lucy Ellinson taking the role of Beth. This version opened at Birmingham Rep on 1 February 2007.

Presumption was presented in association with Sheffield Theatres through the Pyramid Project. Funded by Arts Council England, Yorkshire, and supported by Site Gallery, Sheffield.

A bare stage. Bare, that is, apart from the multiple markings for the positions of furniture, and stuff. Something in between an architect's plan and a crime scene, perhaps.

PART ONE

BETH and TOM enter. They stand on their marks. They talk to the audience.

AMBULANCE STORY

BETH: I nearly got killed today. By an ambulance. The wind was so strong, it was hard to tell where the siren was coming from. What do you call that? The Doppler Effect.

I stepped into the road and it came speeding around the corner. I didn't even have a split second to start stepping back. It was pure luck it didn't hit me. Another centimetre and the wing mirror would have taken my head off for sure.

It wasn't my past that flashed before my eyes, though. It was his future.

Not that I will tell him this, of course. What would be the point? I do love him. But it's just that, sometimes, I wonder if someone else couldn't do a better job if I suddenly wasn't here.

I DON'T NOT LOVE HER

TOM: I don't not love her. Isn't that pathetic?

I don't not love her, and I don't not blame her.

I don't know what to say when we talk about love. Apart from 'I love you'. And that's not nearly enough. We should take evening classes, learn another language. I don't know. Ukrainian, maybe. Or some obscure computer code that bears no relation to anything we might use in the real world.

It just seems wrong at this stage to be talking about love, or its failure, in the same language you'd ask for a cup of tea in. Seven years has devalued language.

I want to beep it at her. Or wave flags. I don't not love you. Is that okay? Tell me something. Anything.

I want to see how this ends now. I want to see if it ends.

I look at her sometimes and I know she dislikes me intensely. She doesn't not love me, but on occasion, not very rare occasion as it happens, she does dislike me. And me her.

I want to tell her that's okay. You can love me and dislike me, after all this time. You can hold those two things in your head. As long as you don't not love me.

It's okay to ask yourself questions, because I do. I do it all the time. Why are we in this house together? Who are you to be in my house, in my arms, in my bed? You resent my presence. It's only natural. I don't feel I have the capacity to surprise you anymore. There's nothing I could possibly do that would seem out of the ordinary.

Is this just how everyone feels? You see a couple. You know them. Solid. Tight, so that you never use one of their names without using the other. And then they split up. An individual unit becomes two individuals. Learning all over again what it means to be alone.

And you just think that. I look at you and I think, is this how everyone feels? Is it just the way it is after so long?

I don't not love you. I don't not know you. I don't even want to think about not loving you or not knowing you. But it is there.

They look at each other for the first time. They smile.

They exit in opposite directions.

TABLE AND CHAIRS

BETH appears from the darkness wearing five wooden dining chairs.

TOM appears carrying a dining table over his head. He stands on his mark, which is surrounded by many smaller marks.

BETH puts the chairs down and extricates herself from them. She takes one and places it into one set of marks on the floor around TOM. She places a second chair. No rush. She gives TOM's stomach a pat.

She places three more chairs on their marks. Stands back, realises, rushes off.

She returns with the sixth chair and positions it behind TOM. She goes round to the chair opposite him, and they sit together, lowering the table into place, perfectly on its marks around the six chairs.

A moment.

BETH: We're sitting in the wrong chairs.

TOM: Yeah.

Without getting up, they reposition the chairs onto different marks, pushed out from the table.

TOM: Shall we?

TOM changes chair. BETH stands and walks away from the table.

INFIDELITY 1

BETH: Was it OK?

          ...

          The food? Was it?

TOM: Hm?

            Yeah. It was fine.

            ...

            I liked it. I like food. Keeps you alive.

BETH: It was good to see everyone.

TOM: They're good people, your friends.

BETH: Your friends too.

BETH places her right hand on the table, as if to move something.

They realise that the table is bare. They exit in opposite directions.

LAYING THE TABLE

TOM brings on tablecloth, lays it in one neat move, sets napkins and tea towels.

BETH brings on crockery, salt and pepper mills and two orange candles.

BETH divides the six plates and six bowls between them, and she and TOM race to place them on the table

They think they're done, but then TOM remembers the cutlery in his pocket. He looks at the table, then scatters the cutlery across it in one throw.

INFIDELITY 2

BETH: Was it OK?

            ...

            The food? Was it?

TOM: Hm?

         …

         Yeah. It was fine.

         …

         I liked it. I like food. Keeps you alive.

BETH: It was good to see everyone.

TOM: They're good people, your friends.

BETH: Your friends too.

BETH moves a spoon with her right hand.

TOM: 'Course.

         …

         Just that you work with them, so it's like –

         …

         Well you know them better, don't you? Better than me.

BETH: Better than you?

TOM: Don't be –

         …

         You know what I mean.

         …

         It's interesting to hear about other people's work, I guess.
         The ins and outs of it. The office politics. I see a different
         side of you.

BETH: Really?

TOM: Yeah. It's like you're a tree falling in the forest.

BETH: You're pissed.

TOM: I'm not. I mean it's like when you're not with me. When you're someone else. If you fall, like that tree, and I'm not there to hear it, do you make a sound?

            ...

            Not that you fall. Not literally. But if you do something, you know? Something that maybe you don't do around me, because I'm never in certain situations with you. Do you really do it? Are you really that person if I'm not there to see you?

            ...

TOM walks away from the table, and points at something that is not there.

            Do you want one of these?

They exchange a look.

BETH: I'll go.

They exit in opposite directions.

CABINET, LIGHTS, WHISKY

Thuds from the wings. BETH emerges from the wings, rolling a huge cabinet on in front of her. She gets it onto its mark.

TOM brings on a whisky bottle and glasses on a tray and sets it on a shelf in the cabinet.

BETH lowers a set of lights down over cabinet.

They stand by the cabinet briefly before returning to the table.

INFIDELITY 3: LINE RUN

They speed through the dialogue that we've already heard:

BETH: Was it OK?

          The food? Was it?

TOM: Hm?

          Yeah. It was fine.

          I liked it. I like food. Keeps you alive.

BETH: It was good to see everyone.

TOM: They're good people, your friends.

BETH: Your friends too.

BETH moves a spoon with her right hand.

TOM: 'Course.

          Just that you work with them, so it's like –

          Well you know them better, don't you? Better than me.

BETH: Better than you?

TOM: Don't be –

          You know what I mean.

          It's interesting to hear about other people's work, I guess.
          The ins and outs of it. The office politics. I see a different
          side of you.

BETH: Really?

TOM: Yeah. It's like you're a tree falling in the forest.

BETH: You're pissed.

TOM: I'm not. I mean it's like when you're not with me. When
          you're someone else. If you fall, like that tree and I'm not
          there to hear it, do you make a sound?

          Not that you fall. Not literally. But if you do something,
          you know? Something that maybe you don't do around
          me, because I'm never in certain situations with you. Do
          you really do it? Are you really that person if I'm not
          there to see you?

TOM goes to cabinet and picks up whisky glass.

Back to normal speed:

          Do you want one of these?

BETH: No, thank you. So you're saying I only exist if you're
          there to see me?

TOM pours himself a whisky and returns to the table.

TOM: No. It's –

          When you're with people I don't normally see you with,
          then I see you act in ways that I don't see. They don't –

          …

          Well I don't. Know they happen. So it's like seeing a
          different you. You laugh differently. Your voice changes.
          You have stronger opinions about people. It's interesting.
          To watch and listen.

BETH: Simon was quiet.

BETH stands and starts to collect napkins and fold them.

TOM: Didn't he just split up with –

TOM walks away from table and stops.

      …

      What was her name?

BETH: Jenny.

He indicates the empty marks where the sofa should sit.

TOM: I'll just be, erm…

      I'll just be a minute. I know where it is.

TOM exits.

BETH un-tidies the napkins and sits back at the table.

SOFA

Muffled swearing from the wings.

TOM struggles on with the sofa, three cushions held in his teeth.

He sets the sofa, then the cushions.

INFIDELITY 4: LINE RUN (WITH MISTAKES)

They try to speed through the dialogue we have already heard:

BETH: Was it OK?

      The food? Was it? –

TOM: Hm?

      Yeah. It was fine.

      I liked it. I like food. Keeps you alive.

BETH: It was good to see everyone.

TOM: They're good people, your friends.

BETH: Your friends too.

BETH moves a spoon with her right hand.

TOM: 'Course.

          Just that you work with them, so it's like –

          Well you know them better, don't you? Better than me.

BETH: You're pissed.

TOM stops.

*A brief improvised discussion: TOM explains to BETH that she has
skipped forward a bit, but that it's not a problem. Then:*

TOM: Well you know them better, don't you? Better than me.

BETH: Better than you?

TOM: Don't be –

          You know what I mean.

          It's interesting to hear about other people's work, I guess.
          The ins and outs of it. The office politics. I see a different
          side of you.

BETH: Really?

TOM: Yeah. It's like you're a tree falling in the forest.

BETH stands and moves round the table to the napkins. TOM stops.

*A brief improvised exchange about whether or not BETH should
be standing up yet. She sits down again. A moment to think, then:*

BETH: You're pissed.

TOM: I'm not. I mean it's like when you're not with me. When you're someone else. If you fall, like that tree and I'm not there to hear it, do you make a sound?

Not that you fall. Not literally. But if you do something, you know? Something...

BETH interrupts and points out that the whisky glass on the table shouldn't be there. A brief improvised discussion about whether this matters or not, at the end of which TOM covers the glass from BETH's eyeline with his hand, then:

Not that you fall. Not literally. But if you do something, you know? Something that maybe you don't do around me, because I'm never in certain situations with you. Do you really do it? Are you really that person if I'm not there to see you?

TOM goes to cabinet pretending not to carry the whisky glass, then holds it up.

Do you want one of these?

BETH: No, thank you. So, you're saying I only exist if you're there to see me?

TOM returns to the table.

TOM: No. It's –

When you're with people I don't normally see you with, then I see you act in ways that I don't see. They don't –

Well I don't. Know they happen. So, it's like seeing a different you. You laugh differently. Your voice changes. You have stronger opinions about people. It's interesting. To watch and listen.

BETH: Simon was quiet.

BETH stands and starts to collect napkins and fold them.

TOM: Didn't he just split up with –

TOM crosses to the sofa and sits.

Back to normal speed.

           What was her name?

BETH: Jenny.

BETH sits at the table.

TOM: Oh. Yeah… He was quiet.

BETH: He's miserable. They were together for a long time.

           …

TOM: What happened?

BETH: You know Jeff?

TOM: No.

BETH: Yes you do. He was Simon's best mate from way back.
           From university.

TOM: Oh.

BETH: Things have been going weird between Simon and
           Jenny for some time. Jenny was being really distant and
           uncommunicative. They were hardly having sex.

TOM: What's weird about that?

BETH: They were never having sex. Simon used to go round to
           Jeff's to talk about it, you know, for support. Apparently,
           Jeff started being really shifty. Shoulder to cry on one
           week, didn't want to listen the next.

...

Fortnight later, Jenny's moved in with Jeff. Simon's lost his fiancée and his best mate.

Oi, feet!

A look. TOM lifts his feet up into the air and holds them there.

BETH exits.

COFFEE TABLE

BETH wheels on coffee table, sitting on it. She spins round and reverses it into place under TOM's feet.

INFIDELITY 5: PLAYFUL

They remain on the sofa and coffee table.

They do the dialogue we've already heard as fast as they can, but have fun with it. In the original production they hammed it up as if super-posh.

BETH: Was it OK?

          The food? Was it? –

TOM: Hm?

          Yeah. It was fine.

          I liked it. I like food. Keeps you alive.

BETH: It was good to see everyone.

TOM: They're good people, your friends.

BETH: Your friends too.

TOM: 'Course.

Just that you work with them, so it's like –

Well you know them better, don't you? Better than me.

BETH: Better than you?

TOM: Don't be –

You know what I mean.

It's interesting to hear about other people's work, I guess. The ins and outs of it. The office politics. I see a different side of you.

BETH: Really?

TOM: Yeah. It's like you're a tree falling in the forest.

BETH: You're pissed.

TOM: I'm not. I mean it's like when you're not with me. When you're someone else. If you fall, like that tree and I'm not there to hear it, do you make a sound?

Not that you fall. Not literally. But if you do something, you know? Something that maybe you don't do around me, because I'm never in certain situations with you. Do you really do it? Are you really that person if I'm not there to see you?

Do you want one of these?

BETH: No, thank you. So you're saying I only exist if you're there to see me?

TOM: No. It's –

When you're with people I don't normally see you with, then I see you act in ways that I don't see. They don't –

Well I don't. Know they happen. So it's like seeing a different you. You laugh differently. Your voice changes.

You have stronger opinions about people. It's interesting. To watch and listen.

BETH: Simon was quiet.

TOM: Didn't he just split up with –

What was her name?

BETH: Jenny.

TOM: Oh. Yeah... He was quiet.

BETH: He's miserable. They were together for a long time.

TOM: What happened?

BETH: You know Jeff?

TOM: No.

BETH: Yes you do. He was Simon's best mate from way back. From university.

TOM: Oh.

BETH: Things have been going weird between Simon and Jenny for some time. Jenny was being really distant and uncommunicative. They were hardly having sex.

TOM: What's weird about that?

BETH: Darling! They were never having sex!

Simon used to go round to Jeff's to talk about it, you know, for support. Apparently, Jeff started being really shifty. Shoulder to cry on one week, didn't want to listen the next.

Fortnight later, Jenny's moved in with Jeff. Simon's lost his fiancée and his best mate.

Darling, feet!

They both take their feet of the furniture.

Back to normal speed and intonation.

TOM: That's fucked.

          …

          Full marks to him, though. For not talking about it.
          That's the kind of thing you could really monopolise a
          conversation with.

BETH: Well. As long as it didn't get in the way of a nice evening.

TOM: You know what I mean.

          …

          If that happened to you and me, I'm not sure I wouldn't
          just go on about it, for… a bit.

BETH returns to the table and tidying the napkins.

BETH: It's hardly likely, is it? Me running off with your best
          mate.

          …

          Is it?

TOM: No.

          Makes you think, though.

          I mean, if I suddenly. I don' know. If I suddenly turned
          round to you and said I was having an affair. I mean
          totally hypothetically. If you found out, or if I told you –

BETH: I need a drink.

BETH exits.

WINE GLASSES

BETH brings on tray bearing a full wine bottle and 10 glasses.

TOM looks up, stands and crosses to the table.

BETH sits on the sofa and pours different amounts of wine into each glass. She puts the empty bottle on the coffee table and the tray underneath.

She picks up the first glass – half-full.

BETH: This, this is my glass of wine, I poured it at the end of a party; a dinner party that he didn't want to have. But I persuaded him on the grounds that we wouldn't have a starter and I'd do the clearing up.

            Cheers.

She puts down the glass and picks up the next one – nearly empty.

            This one is his. He's had five, six, seven, eight, I've lost count. He's on the whisky now. And the next four...

She moves the next four glasses – mostly empty – into pairs.

            ... belong to the guests.

She picks up the next one – half-full – and changes position on the sofa.

            I'm gulping this down. I'm in the bedroom and I'm crying. We've had a bit of an argument. Actually it wasn't an argument, that's entirely the point. I just wanted to get a response out of him. Any sort of response at all. I wanted him to be as emotional as me. So I hit him. I smacked him across the face and he didn't do anything. He just sat there and looked at me. So I did it again. And again. He didn't try to stop me. He defended himself, but he just looked at me. And I couldn't stand it and I was crying, so I left the room. And I got this bottle and I'm in here and I'll probably finish it.

She puts down the glass and picks up the next one – too full – and again finds a different position on the sofa.

I shouldn't have poured this. I insisted on opening the bottle. We've come in from the pub and we are absolutely rat-arsed and in a minute he's going to come in and he's gonna lean over and he's gonna try and kiss me and he's going to fall onto the sofa, we are both going to roll onto the floor, the coffee table's gonna be pushed and I'm gonna be laid there thinking it's the most romantic thing… And he's going to start moaning about getting carpet burns. And we'll move into the bedroom but we won't take our clothes off, we'll fall asleep and this lot will get cleared away in the morning.

She puts down the glass, picks up the next one – a third full – changes position.

I don't think I can finish this. It's drifting out of focus. I'm in a restaurant, having lunch with a girlfriend of mine. I can't really make out what she is saying. I've just been to the toilet. It's a stupid time to do it, I do realise that, but I had to know. I'm impatient. So I went and I sat staring at that cream oval, waiting to see if the little blue cross would appear. I sat thinking, well, I just think that it would be more like a death sentence, than the start of something. All I can think is we're not ready for this, that there's loads of things that I want to do. And we've not been together for that long and this would just be something that would get in the way. And as I stared, looking at that cream oval this goes over and over in my mind, until slowly just one blue line appears. So I come back to the restaurant, and I am sitting opposite my friend and I can't tell her what I've just done, because I can't help feeling a little disappointed.

She puts down the glass and picks up the next one – half-full.

I didn't expect to be drinking this, not at this time of the day, anyway. But then you don't usually get that kind of phone call. The voice on the other end of the phone was telling me stuff. Saying things like, 'Too young.' And all I could think was, why have I not seen her since school? I knew that I should say something, but I couldn't. There I was on the phone in silence.

And then after a while the voice started speaking again, telling me that there was a funeral, would I go?

I once read that you can't truly start to live your life until you know for sure when it is going to end: there's a set time frame. And I'm really glad I don't know that about myself. But I can't help wondering if it would change things if I did.

She puts down the glass and takes four other glasses (3–6) to the table.

She returns for the first two glasses – puts one in front of TOM, takes the other one herself. She sits in the wrong chair with her back to him.

INFIDELITY 6: PISSED OFF

They run the text we've already heard as fast as they can, as an argument.

BETH: Was it OK?

          The food? Was it?

TOM: Hm?

          Yeah. It was fine.

          I liked it. I like food. Keeps you alive.

BETH: It was good to see everyone.

TOM: They're good people, your friends.

BETH: Your friends too.

TOM: 'Course.

Just that you work with them, so it's like –

Well you know them better, don't you? Better than me.

BETH: Better than you?

TOM: Don't be –

You know what I mean.

It's interesting to hear about other people's work, I guess. The ins and outs of it. The office politics. I see a different side of you.

BETH: Really?

TOM: Yeah. It's like you're a tree falling in the forest.

BETH: You're pissed.

TOM: I'm not. I mean it's like when you're not with me. When you're someone else. If you fall, like that tree and I'm not there to hear it, do you make a sound?

Not that you fall. Not literally. But if you do something, you know? Something that maybe you don't do around me, because I'm never in certain situations with you. Do you really do it? Are you really that person if I'm not there to see you?

Do you want one of these?

BETH: No, thank you. So you're saying I only exist if you're there to see me?

TOM: No. It's –

When you're with people I don't normally see you with, then I see you act in ways that I don't see. They don't –

Well I don't. Know they happen. So it's like seeing a different you. You laugh differently. Your voice changes. You have stronger opinions about people. It's interesting. To watch and listen.

BETH: Simon was quiet.

TOM: Didn't he just split up with –

What was her name?

BETH: Jenny.

TOM: Oh. Yeah… He was quiet.

BETH: He's miserable. They were together for a long time.

TOM: What happened?

BETH: You know Jeff?

TOM: No.

BETH: Yes you do. He was Simon's best mate from way back. From university.

TOM: Oh.

BETH: Things have been going weird between Simon and Jenny for some time. Jenny was being really distant and uncommunicative. They were hardly having sex.

TOM: What's weird about that?

BETH: They were never having sex. Simon used to go round to Jeff's to talk about it, you know, for support. Apparently, Jeff started being really shifty. Shoulder to cry on one week, didn't want to listen the next.

Fortnight later, Jenny's moved in with Jeff. Simon's lost his fiancée and his best mate.

TOM: That's fucked. Full marks to him though. For not talking about it. That's the kind of thing you could really monopolise a conversation with.

BETH: Well. As long as it didn't get in the way of a nice evening.

TOM: You know what I mean. If that happened to you and me, I'm not sure I wouldn't just go on about it. For a bit.

BETH: It's hardly likely, is it? Me running off with your best mate. Is it?

TOM: No.

TOM stands up and crosses to the sofa and sits.

Back to normal speed and intonation.

Makes you think, though.

I mean, if I suddenly. I don't know. If I suddenly turned round to you and said I was having an affair. I mean totally hypothetically. If you found out, or if I told you –

BETH: Which?

...

If I found out or if you told me?

TOM: Would it make a difference?

BETH: Yes.

TOM: I'd have had the affair. I'd have done the same wrong however you found out.

BETH: I suppose.

TOM: But if I'd... Not a one-night stand, but a relationship. Something regular. With someone else.

...

Just hypothetically. Just throwing it in the air.

...

What d'you think you'd do?

...

BETH: I'd leave.

...

No. First I'd text and email everyone you know personally and professionally to tell them all what an utter twat you are. Then I'd change the locks so it would take you ages to get into the flat, only to discover, when you did, that I wasn't there.

TOM: You'd just go?

You wouldn't even want to try?

BETH: No.

...

I don't know.

I don't think so.

...

What would be the point? I don't think I could see a way back from that. After knowing what you'd done with someone else. That you'd lied to be there as well.

...

I don't think I could. I mean wouldn't you leave me if I did the same?

Hypothetically?

TOM: Don't think I would, no.

BETH: Really?

TOM: Really.

BETH: Bollocks.

TOM: No.

BETH: Oh, c'mon, think about it.

BETH stands, crosses to TOM and puts her hands out, as if to lean on something.

BOTH: Oh for fuck's sake.

TOM: I'll get it.

          Do you want to... you know...?

TOM exits.

BETH crosses to the table.

INFIDELITY 7: SUMMARY

Semi-improvised:

BETH: Right, okay! Well, you know this. There is a... table and
          six chairs, I sit here and he sits there... I ask him if he
          likes the food, he says something sarcastic: 'he likes food
          it keeps him alive', he's pissed and starts going on about
          being a tree in a forest or something...

TOM brings on armchair. He sets it whilst BETH continues:

          Anyway, he offers me drink and I say no thank you and
          then I tell him about friends of ours Simon, Jenny and
          Jeff, Simon and Jenny have split up recently, it's been
          pretty dreadful you know so...

TOM: I get a drink and I sit over here...

TOM sits on the sofa.

And she starts talking about Simon and Jenny and Jeff
and there's been an affair and Jenny's run off with Jeff
and so I ask her what she'd do if I was having an affair
and she says

BETH: I'd leave

TOM: She'd leave, and then she turns it around and asks me,
if I found out she was having an affair, wouldn't I leave
her? And I say...

Back to normal delivery.

I don't think I would, no.

BETH: Really?

TOM: Really.

BETH: Bollocks.

TOM: No.

BETH: Oh, c'mon, think about it.

*BETH stands up and comes forward, putting her hands on the
back of the armchair.*

I'm screwing someone else. Letting someone else stick their
dick in me. And you're telling me you wouldn't walk away?

BETH sits in the armchair.

TOM: It depends.

BETH: On what, for fuck's sake?

TOM: I mean if you were. If you'd fallen I don't know, head
          over heels in love with them. With this other bloke –

BETH: Ah, could be a woman.

TOM: Wouldn't mind that so much, as long as you let me watch.

BETH demonstrates her exasperation with this comment.

TOM: But if you. If you were in love with them and not with
          me. Well there'd be nothing I could do about that. But if
          it was a symptom of something. Something going wrong
          that we could fix. Or try to fix. I don't think I'd go. Not
          straight away. Until we'd tried to sort whatever it was
          out.

BETH: So you're saying, I could theoretically go to bed with
          whomever I like as long as I didn't love them?

TOM: No…

BETH: I find that very hard to believe.

TOM: Like I said. If it was a symptom –

BETH: Symptom my arse.

TOM goes to the cabinet.

          I don't think you'd do that. I think you'd walk. And if
          you didn't you'd either be a saint or a pushover. And you
          being either of those things. Well it'd irritate me so much
          that I'd probably have to leave before I fucking killed you.

Pouring himself another whisky:

TOM: Okay…

          …

Well suppose I'd had an affair. But a long time ago.

BETH: How long?

TOM: Oh. Five years?

          ...

          But you'd only just found out about it.

BETH: Five years ago?

TOM: Yeah. Nothing major.

          Well major, obviously, because it's an affair. But not that long. A few weeks, maybe. A month, say. Just something that happened and then stopped happening. More of a fling, really. For a month or so. Five years ago.

BETH: This is getting worryingly specific now, Tom.

TOM goes to the chair and kisses BETH's head.

TOM: I'm just. It's just an imaginary situation, okay?

He moves round to sit on the sofa.

BETH: Okay. And I didn't know about it then.

TOM: No. You only found out about it now. Tomorrow, say. Years later. When it's all done and finished. Ancient history.

BETH: Then why choose to tell me tomorrow?

TOM: Maybe I don't tell you. Maybe you just find out. A conversation at a party or something. You piece it together. Doesn't matter how. The important thing is –

BETH: So I find out about some fling you had five years ago.

...

You're asking, what would I do?

TOM: No. Well, I don't know what you'd do. So I'm asking that, yeah. But what I'm also asking is, does that fling make the subsequent five years we've spent together a lie? Even though nothing else has happened since?

BETH: I'm starting to really dislike this conversation.

BETH stands and crosses to the table.

TOM: I'm just talking.

BETH: Are you?

TOM: Jesus, yeah.

...

Do you never think about this stuff?

BETH: About what?

About fucking around?

...

About you fucking around?

TOM: Not that. Not specifically –

...

Just. All the what-ifs that start to pile up after all this time. We've got a shitload of them, I guess. This is just one...

BETH starts to collect the wine glasses from the table

So?

BETH: So I don't know, Tom. Are you seriously asking me to weigh
           up the implications of some theoretical affair with some
           non-existent other woman against a seven-year relationship
           in all of, what? Thirty seconds?

TOM: Just. If you found out –

BETH: I don't know.

TOM: It never happened.

BETH: That's hardly the point.

           …

           The point is, Tom –

           I don't know.

She begins to leave.

           You're sitting in the dark.

BETH exits.

TWO PEOPLE

TOM: There are two people of different genders…

           There's a man and a woman and they live together in
           a flat, surrounded by all their stuff. And they've been
           together for a long time and independently, without talking,
           they have both started asking the same question, or

He drinks one of the glasses of wine left on the coffee table.

           rather, wondering how a statement can turn into a question,
           they are wondering how 'I love you' has turned into

He drinks a second glass of wine.

'why do I love you?' and in turn, how 'why do I love you?'

He drinks the third glass of wine.

> has turned into, 'is it enough, to love you?' and the
> answer to that is, the answer is,

He drinks the last glass of wine.

> they don't know.

GOING TO BED

BETH brings on a standard lamp, places it next to the sofa, on its mark, plugs it in and switches it on.

She stands by the armchair.

BETH: I come back into the room and I say, 'I'm going to go to
          bed now.'

TOM: Oh, right.

BETH: And then I hover here for longer than is necessary, and
          then I say, 'well are you coming?'

TOM: I think I'm just going to stay up in here for a bit, I'm not
          really that tired.

BETH: 'Right', I say and then I walk across the room as though
          I'm about to leave –

BETH crosses to behind the table.

> But then I stop halfway and turn and I just can't help
> myself and I say, 'well how long are you going to be
> then? I mean shall I leave the light on, hall light on,
> you know shall I read, what?'

TOM: Well, I don't know, I'll come to bed when I'm tired,
          you switch the light off, it's going to keep you awake
          otherwise, if I need to read I'll do it in here.

BETH: And I don't want to go to bed now, because he's not
          going to bed, but I've got to go to bed because I've said
          that I am going to bed. 'Well, I'll see you in the morning
          then,' I say.

TOM: Yeah, well you'll see me in bed.

BETH: 'Yeah, well I'll be asleep then wont I?' I say.

TOM: Fair enough.

BETH: And then I leave. I go into the bedroom.

BETH exits.

TOM sits on the sofa.

Eventually he turns the lamp off. Blackout.

PART TWO

The lights come up. TOM has gone. The lighting and sound suggest that this is the following morning.

TABLECLOTH, PHONE & DESK

BETH enters and begins to clear away the dishes. After moving a few plates, she stops and grabs all four corners of the tablecloth and bundles all of the dinner stuff up inside it. She lifts it all off the table and looks around.

As she moves towards the cabinet, the phone starts to ring. She stuffs the tablecloth into the cabinet and exits.

The phone rings.

BETH returns, holding the phone. She goes to place it, only to see that the desk isn't there.

TOM brings on desk, places it, then exits.

BETH holds the ringing phone.

TOM returns with the desk props in a bin. He takes the props out of the bin and sets them on the desk: radio, lamp, laptop, letter holder, pad, pen holder with pencils and pens, photo frame. Sets the bin next to desk. He tears the top sheet of the pad, crumples it up, puts it in the bin. Exits.

Returns with the chair, sets it under the desk, pauses briefly, then resets it in its other set of marks and sits on it.

BETH puts the telephone on the edge of desk, puts the cable in drawer and stands next to desk.

TELEPHONE CONVERSATION

The phone is still ringing. BETH lets out a cry of frustration and answers it.

BETH: Hello? Oh hiya! You all right? Yeah, yeah, he's here, yep, just a second. It's er... It's for you.

TOM: Who is it?

BETH: It's me.

TOM: Oh, right...

Takes the phone.

Hello you. Oh all right then well... yeah... I mean well... I mean if you are only going to be like one maybe a couple of hours late then just say 'cause I'll hang on for you. Oh, okay if it's a work thing that's fine. No it's. No. No if you can't say how long you are going to be. Look I'll tell you what then, I'll just make something and leave some out for you... well just tell me what you want and I'll go out and get that... okay then tell me what you don't want and I'll go out and not get that... Well I could... look, hang on a sec...

BETH has been trying to get TOM's attention.

BETH: Why are you giving me a hard time?

TOM: I'm not giving you a hard time, I'm just asking what you want for your dinner...

BETH: You are. I've been polite enough to phone up and say that I'm going to be late and all of a sudden it's turned into the Spanish fucking Inquisition.

TOM: It's not turned into any kind of fucking Inquisition. It's just that if you were going to be late home, then I was offering to make you some tea so that you weren't hungry.

BETH: Yeah, but the point is, that I don't want any tea, do I? I don't want to have to phone up, I don't want to have to be here at a certain time every night to sit down at that table and have some food with you.

TOM: Well you don't have to be, we don't have that kind of routine do we, you're making me out to be some sort of tea fetishist now... I was just offering to make you some tea if you were going to be late so you don't have to go to bed hungry...

BETH: ... Okay fine.

BETH crosses to armchair. She sits and picks up the glass of whisky.

TOM turns his attention back to the phone.

TOM: Sorry about that. Yeah, yeah okay, yeah well if you find out what time, just call me or text me or something, yeah, okay, yep, you too.

TOM puts down receiver. He stays at the desk, and eventually turns his attention to a book on the desk.

PHILIP

BETH: Philip. The reason why I phoned to say I'd be late, his name is Philip. We're having a drink – a meeting – about the possibility of some freelance work, and while we are talking it dawns on me that some of the less informed people in this bar might at a cursory glance think that we are a couple. And that makes me feel like an impostor, but at the same time the novelty of the situation quite excites me.

She stands, leaning on the arm of the armchair.

Every now and again I review things between him and me; the state of play. Well you do, don't you? In the first week of a romance you ask yourself every hour; is that person right for me? Then it becomes every week, then you have your Six-Month Review, and then after that it just tends to be when you have an argument or some sort of life event jerks you out of your comfort zone that you are so busy nesting away at. And at that time I ask myself, do I love him? And, how much? And then I think through the alternatives or a possible exit strategy and it comes down to a number of points.

Number one: I do not want to be alone.

Two: I'd have to completely relearn how to meet people, and going back to square one scares the shit out of me. I've not been there for a long time.

Three: stuff. We've got shared insurance, joint accounts, amenity bills in both names, boxes of photographs that we never look at, CDs, books, donor cards and passports where the other is named the next of kin. We've got the furniture and the TV and the stereo and the flat. A lot of these things I just can't afford to give up or I wouldn't want to live without.

Four: laziness. Short cuts. I don't know, expectations? You have to put in a lot of hours to get to know someone, a lot of investment. Comfortable silences take time.

Five: well that's kids. I want them. I think. I don't know. I think that maybe I do want them, but I know that my chances of finding out diminish rapidly the moment I walk out that door. So I go through this and I reach the conclusion that I do love him. Enough. To not have to go through any of those things or give any of them up. And I also know that at the end of the evening I'll finish my drink with Philip, and I'll just go home.

She slides backwards into the armchair.

FUCKING LIBERAL GUILT

TOM: Fucking liberal guilt. I'm worried about my relationship. I'm fully aware that's a luxury. I've purchased the head-space that I use to worry about my relationship. I've purchased it with fair trade coffee and recycled plastic. I've purchased it with a ten-pound standing order every month that will apparently once and for all stop people having sex with children. I've purchased it by thinking really hard about what it would be like to be chained to a radiator in Baghdad or to watch as my subsistence farm is deprived of water to provide electricity for casinos and strip joints a thousand miles away. I've purchased it by putting money in various hats, but only hats that I've first confirmed are made of ethically sourced sustainable materials and not put together by children working under inadequate labour laws.

My concern is entirely passive, it's just a series of computerised transactions designed to make me feel less guilty about fretting. To give me that little five-minute window, that five-minute guilt holiday each day when I can put my fingers into the cracks of my relationship, and just push them slightly wider, instead of doing what most of the people in this world have got to do with their lives which is get the fuck on with them. I feel guilty about having no worries. I honestly think I'd like some. I honestly think that my love would be more instinctive, less relentlessly questioned, just deeper, if there was a serious chance I might contract cholera or get smart-bombed or that my neighbours might come round and machine gun me into a shallow grave in the name of religion. Because when you think about it, you know, people who live in war zones, they must have that whole relationship thing pretty much sorted, mustn't they?

ORNAMENTS

TOM slowly returns his attention to the desk.

BETH swings her legs over the armchair and stands. She looks at the furniture, then exits.

TOM starts working at the desk.

BETH returns with cabinet props, exiting and returning several times, until the cabinet shelves are full of magazine racks, boxes of CDs and cassette tapes, baskets, soda siphon, glasses, camera and vases.

TOM starts wandering around the flat, distracted.

BETH places a magazine rack by the sofa.

TOM lies on the sofa and takes a magazine from the rack.

BETH places candles on the dining table.

TOM returns to the desk, tries to work.

BETH brings on a louvre style screen and sets it in the corner. She peeks behind, then emerges from behind it. She resets cushions, checks the screen then crosses to TOM.

She creeps up on him, tickles him then puts her arms around him and kisses him.

BETH: You know if you go and get the cupboard it will be two days later.

TOM: ...

          Oh, yeah, right.

They both exit.

TOM brings on a mid-height cupboard, puts it on its mark. He takes a vase out of it and fills it with water from a bottle that is also in the cupboard. He closes the cupboard door and waits.

BETH enters with a bag and a bunch of flowers.

DO THE MATHS (PART 1 – FRIDGE)

BETH: Hello you.

BETH crosses to TOM and kisses him.

TOM: Hiya.

           …

           They for me?

BETH: Oh no. No, they are already here.

She puts the flowers in the vase.

BETH: So… what have you been doing?

TOM: Just working, well I say working, I was working for a bit…

BETH turns to put her bag down.

BETH: Sorry… hang on…

TOM: What?

BETH: I'll be back in a minute…

TOM: It's okay – I should be…

BETH exits. TOM lies on sofa.

BETH brings on a large basket, sets it in front of screen, exits, returns.

BETH: Hello you.

She stops when she sees TOM is not by the cupboard.

TOM: Hiya.

BETH goes to the sofa, kisses TOM then drops her bag in the basket.

BETH: How you doing?

TOM: Fine.

BETH: What have you been doing?

BETH slides over the back of the sofa to lie with TOM just as TOM gets up and starts pacing.

TOM: I was working, well, well, I say I was working. I actually got distracted.

BETH: Really.

BETH takes her shoes off and makes herself comfortable on the sofa. TOM continues to pace.

TOM: Yeah, I was listening this programme on the radio, it was one of those you know kind of factoid programmes about, well this one was about how many hours you spend in your life doing certain things, you know if you were to take all that time as a block, you know, like weeks reading or weeks or months hopefully having sex, or you know on holiday, or whatever yeah. And that's all fine all well and good, but there was just one thing that got stuck in my head, right, which is apparently, right, did you know, right, if you took all the time together, during the whole of your life, you will spend 38 days looking for stuff in the fridge.

BETH: 38 days?

TOM: 38 days. So I started thinking about that 38 days spread out over our whole lives and the proportion before we were together and then after we were together and should we live to a ripe old age, you know like eighty-six or eighty-seven or something, what proportion of that 38 days would be within our relationship and I worked out, that in our relationship, at the end of it, you and I will both have spent 30 days looking for jam in the fridge.

BETH: Yeah, but I don't like jam, do I?

TOM: Jam, Marmite whatever.

BETH: You don't put Marmite in the fridge.

TOM: I know you don't put Marmite in the fridge. Marmalade! Whatever! That's not the point! It just made me think about time. And I started thinking about a relationship being made up of units of time and I thought what's the base unit of time for a relationship and I thought well, a week's too long, so an hour, an hour because it's not too short and not too long. I thought about that first hour that we ever spent together, you know as a couple, you know we went to that pub, didn't we?

BETH: Oh God, yeah.

TOM: Yeah, it was shit, my fault, but we got over it. It doesn't matter. The point is, that hour, at the time constituted one hundred percent of our time together. It was the entirety of our relationship, yeah?

BETH: Yeah.

TOM: That hour was everything.

BETH: Yes.

TOM: Now yesterday afternoon we spent an hour just fucking around in the flat, yeah, you were reading the paper, I don't even know what I was doing. We didn't particularly talk to each other or anything. And we've been together what, give or take, seven years, for the purposes of this calculation, let's say seven years exactly. And so I sat down and I worked out that that hour that we spent in this flat yesterday afternoon was 1/61,362 of our entire relationship. That is less than 0.00002%. First hour 100%, yesterday afternoon, a miniscule amount.

BETH: Wow.

TOM: And every hour that passes is a smaller and smaller proportion of our relationship than the one that's gone before. So I started thinking about how that hour, that base unit, depreciates and devalues in all the time we have been together and what that hour meant at the different stages in the time that we've been a couple, yeah? And I thought about the first time we went on holiday together, we'd been together what, about a year?

BETH: Fourteen months.

TOM: Fourteen months, right. And I thought what an hour meant at that point when we'd been together for a year and...

TOM turns to where the bookcase should be.

          I dug out those old photographs.

          I'll just be a minute...

TOM exits.

BOOKSHELVES

TOM brings on bookshelves and places them.

TOM: And I dug out those old photographs.

TOM looks at the empty bookshelves.

Could you come and stand over here for a minute please?

BETH: I'll just put my shoes on.

BETH puts her shoes back on, then crosses to the shelves.

TOM: Just stand here, well where I was stood… okay?

TOM exits.

A single paperback book flies on from the wings.

Then a second. BETH catches it.

BETH catches two shelves' worth of single books, as TOM throws them on from offstage. She rapidly puts them into the bookcase.

Then the books come on in blocks of about ten books stuck together, until another three shelves are full.

Then the ornaments, which BETH catches and places. In the original production this included:

A globe, two photo albums, a wooden ornament from a trip abroad, a pack of cards, tiddlywinks, a framed photo, a toffee tin, a pad, a pencil holder followed by pencils, two baskets of photos and finally a sewing box.

DO THE MATHS (PART 2 – WHEN WE ARE OLD)

TOM and BETH start to clear up dropped books and pencils, and organise the shelves. TOM helps until he takes over the summary, which is semi-improvised.

BETH: So, I get in from work and I ask him how's he been doing and he says, 'yeah okay', only he's not been doing any work, he's been listening to some radio programme about time, blocks of time, and what you do with them, like how long you spend cleaning the car, or having sex in the fridge… or something…

TOM: So, she comes in and asks me what I've been doing and I
            say 'working, well I say working but I got distracted by a
            radio show I was listening to about time, the amount of time
            you spend in life doing various things' and I say 'it made
            me think about how time works in a relationship, the base
            unit being an hour, and about how that hour depreciates
            and devalues' and then I say 'it made me think about the
            first hour we spent together, all our relationship, and about
            yesterday afternoon when the hour meant almost nothing
            and that made me think about what that hour meant at
            various points when we've been together and I thought
            about the first time we went on holiday together after about

BETH: fourteen months

TOM: and I say 'it made me think about what an hour meant then'
            and I say...

            'so, I went, and I dug out some old photographs'...

*TOM picks up a photo album; BETH looks at the pictures with him.
For a moment, they forget we're there.*

            And then I talk about the thing I suppose which disturbed
            me,

TOM moves to his mark, BETH continues to tidy.

            Which was, what the programme made me think about
            was what it'll be like when we are old, you know when we
            are in our mid-to-late seventies even our eighties. We're still
            together. We're in a cottage in the country, with white hair
            and blankets over our legs and what an hour will seem like
            then when we've got for definite less time in front of us
            than we have behind us and even say three or four years
            left at that point will be a tiny proportion of our relationship,
            when it seems quite a huge span of time now. I tell her
            about how it makes me think about what time will be like
            when we are that old together and that inevitably one of us
            will die first and the other one will be left alone and equally
            inevitably there will come a point in our relationship, even

though we won't know it, when we have less than one month left together, and at that point, I will have spent more time during our relationship than we have left together, looking for stuff in the fucking fridge.

And then I look at the photo and a take a deep breath as though I'm about to say something; and it's a bit like...

TOM holds his breath.

BETH has finished tidying.

BETH: It's a bit like he's about to say something like...

   What if I had slept with her on our second date like I wanted to?
   What if her parents really do hate me?
   What if she has thousands of pounds of debt and she's never told me?
   What if I find out in the future that I'm infertile?
   What if we'd got a dog that time we said we would?
   What if she finds God? Or Allah? Or Yahweh? Or Satan?
   What if one day, the doorbell rings and there stands a man, a bit taller than me, saying 'Daddy'?
   What if I lose my genitals in an accident with a revolving door?
   What if she gets Alzheimer's and I forget who we've been?
   What if one of us gives up caffeine?
   What if I say I do and I don't?
   What if I have to manage her pain by putting morphine into her scrambled egg?
   What if we end up just not liking each other very much?
   What if...?

TOM lets out his breath. He returns the photo album its shelf.

TOM: And then I take the photographs back to the bookshelves, I put them away. And we don't mention them again.

BETH goes to the sofa and lies down facing TOM. TOM sits at the dining table.

DO THE MATHS (PART 3 – OUR COTTAGE)

BETH: This cottage of ours in the country sounds nice.

TOM: I say, 'Yeah, it is nice.'

BETH: Does it have a garden?

TOM: And I say, 'Yeah of course it has a garden. A lawn, flowerbeds and a vegetable patch, and maybe some fruit trees.'

BETH: And a stream running through the garden?

TOM: And I say, 'Yeah, and solar panels, so we'll be self-sufficient.'

BETH: A guest room, will we have a guest room?

TOM: And I say, 'Yeah, there'll be plenty of room for guests.' Then I say, 'and there'll be robots to help with the domestic chores we can't be bothered doing.'

BETH: Robots?

TOM: I say 'Yeah, robots, because it'll be the future.'

        …

BETH: Tom. You know how every single minute of our relationship is precious…?

TOM: And I say 'yeah.'

BETH: How do you feel about using the next three minutes of our relationship to make me a cup of tea?

TOM: Go on then

BETH: Thank you.

TOM exits.

LOVE HIDING

BETH arranges the cushions on the sofa.

She returns to the table and resets the chairs on their original marks.

She sits side-in in a chair facing the audience, with her back to the table.

BETH: Love creeps up on you and puts her hand across your eyes, and asks you to guess who she is.

At the same time, she arranges to meet you in a pub. At the same time, she falls screaming from above like a badly prepared skydiver and pile-drives you six feet into the ground.

And sometimes she'll just sit quietly, watching you, waiting for you to notice.

And maybe I'm getting close to working out why we're doing this. We're trying to make love visible again.

It's just she's been sitting quietly in this flat for so long, and in all the other places we are. She's not gone, but invisible. But she's changed shape. She fits in so well between him and me, against the shape of the things we own, that I have to strain to make her out at all. She's still there, in silence, argument, in bed, the books on the shelf, the food in the fridge. But she's so mixed in, so integrated with the look, the flavour of things that it's hard to see or taste her alone anymore. She's another colour on the palette. Another spice in the stew.

She's not gone.

But I want her back.

TOM comes on with mugs of tea. He places BETH's mug on the table in front of her, then sits opposite her.

BETH turns in to the table to face him.

They drink their tea.

The lights slowly fade to black.

The set at the Crucible Studio in 2015. Photo: Martin Fuller.

Chris Thorpe. Photo: Mark Cohen.

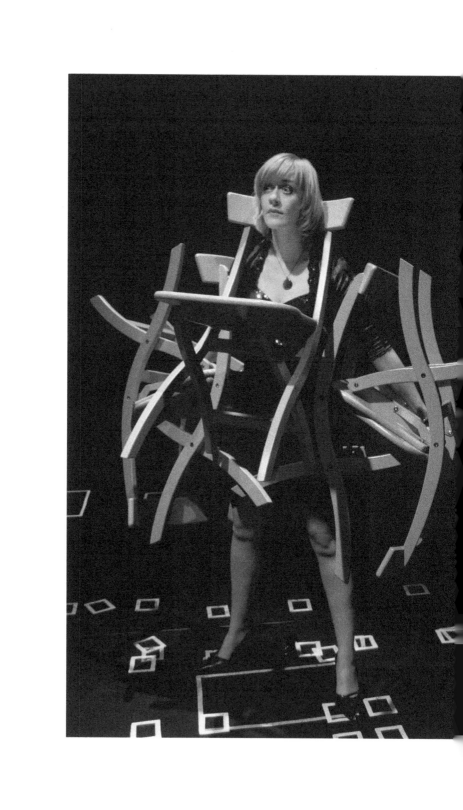

Lucy Ellinson. Photo: Mark Cohen.

Alexander Kelly in *What I Heard About the World*, Sheffield 2010.
Photo: Craig Fleming.

WHAT I HEARD ABOUT THE WORLD

Performance text by
Jorge Andrade
Alexander Kelly
Chris Thorpe
with
José Capela
Rachael Walton

A Conversation About Fake Things

What I Heard About the World was born during a conversation in Jorge Andrade's flat in Lisbon in 2007. Since we had met in 2004 we had been talking about our two companies, Third Angel and mala voadora,[1] collaborating on a project. As is often the way, we had had a moment of realisation that this collaboration was not going to happen unless we actually, you know, started it. (We had had a similar realisation about working with Chris Thorpe a couple of years previously). So, Jorge and Alex met for coffee, each bringing a few ideas to the table. Jorge talked about several newspaper stories that had caught his attention recently. The sort of stories that we would call 'And Finally' stories in the UK. Quirky, would-you-believe-it? stories.

One was about how in Germany you can hire people to turn up at demonstrations for you – to make up the numbers and do some shouting.

Another was about how the number one pastime for off duty US soldiers serving in Iraq or Afghanistan was to play war games – first person simulations set in real wars. Simpler wars, perhaps.

Another was about the Flat Daddies, a US military programme providing life-size cardboard cut-outs of servicemen and women to their families when they go abroad. And the amazing thing in the story, we thought, was that there are documented cases where kids will not speak to their real dads on the phone when they call from abroad, because they have bonded with their flat dads.

It occurred to us that Jorge was collecting stories of fakes and replacements, of substitutes and stand-ins, from around the world.

1   For more about mala voadora's work, visit them at www.malavoadora.pt.

The conversation moved on to maps and mapping, the theme Alex had brought to the meeting. He talked about the map of the USA he had on his bedroom wall as a child. A brightly coloured, illustrated map: each state was coloured in differently, and was represented by a single, hand-drawn icon.[2] We talked about how a map is a fake, or a stand-in. We began discussing a project that located these stories of the inauthentic on a giant map of the world. By the end of the conversation we understood what we thought the project was about, and we had the title, *What I Heard About the World*.

In the months that followed, we continued to build Jorge's collection of stories, pinning them to the map, like butterflies. And the challenge seemed clear: could we find a story of a fake thing, a replacement, or substitute, for every country in the world? We set about looking for commissioners and funding.

Better Words Than 'Fake'

At the start of 2010 mala voadora and Third Angel went public with our search for stories of fakes. Third Angel had made several projects out of collected stories previously, but they had always been personal stories, sourced close to home.[3] This was a distinct widening of our net, looking for stories from countries all around the world. After several conversations and emails checking exactly what it was we were looking for, we clarified something for ourselves and our would-be contributors in a blogpost:

2   Digging out the map during the process of making the show, Alex discovered that actually there are more drawings on it than that – but they are all circular, badge-like illustrations indicating what is the notable feature of that part of the country.

3   *Class of '76* (2000) was made up of stories from Alex's infant school classmates. *The Lad Lit Project* (2005) was built out of stories from men who were close to the team making the show.

This has confirmed our suspicion that we're not particularly interested in deception – in fakes, in hoaxes, in cons. (I am interested in all that stuff, actually, but it's not what I think this show is about). So perhaps 'fake' isn't the right work. Checking 'fake' in a thesaurus just produces more words that imply deception, and in fact some of the other words suggested early on might be more helpful. So, how's this:

We're looking for instances where a replica, substitute, simulation or stand-in is used knowingly, in place of the real thing. An alternative, a deputy, a locum, a proxy. An understudy, even. A deliberate, or at least recognised, reliance on the inauthentic. Things that keep us one step removed from the original. Things that might, in the longer term, replace the original. My instinct tells me that this is not a good thing, but of course research so far has thrown up several examples of instances when this is a really positive thing. And of course, as ever, we are looking for ideas that support and challenge our thesis.

Anything that our impetus suggests to you, we're interested to hear.

In April 2010 we gathered to start working with some of the stories we had collected. Alex and Jorge were joined by Chris Thorpe, who we invited following our collaborations on *Presumption* (2006) and *Parts For Machines That Do Things* (2009). Having heard Chris sing as part of his warm-ups on tour, we also asked him if he would also provide a soundtrack for the show as part of his role. At some point we started referring to the show as a 'theatre piece with songs'.

We were still thinking of the task of the show as collecting at least one story of a substitute or a stand-in for every country. We had an ambition that in the show we would name every country of the world, using the name that the people who live there use, rather than the name that we in the UK or Portugal know it as. We looked at a map. We looked on the internet. We were not able to figure out how many countries there are. So we went to talk to some cartographers.

A Conversation with Worldmapper

In 2009 we had discovered the work of Worldmapper in an exhibition at Sheffield's Millennium Gallery. Their exhibit was a continually morphing world map, in which the sizes and shapes of countries changed to reflect their relative populations, or military spending, or number of nurses, and so on. It was beautiful to watch, whilst at the same time being informative and educational – making complex data really clear through a simple, visual mechanism.[4] We approached them about being part of the project. In April 2010, we went in to the University of Sheffield, where they were then largely based, to meet Danny Dorling, Benjamin Hennig and Anna Barford from the Worldmapper team. We had questions we wanted to ask them, but also, we wanted to tell them what we were planning to do and see what questions this prompted them to ask us.

This was the first of a series of collaborative conversations with Worldmapper that had a profound effect on the direction of the project – although not in the direction anticipated.

4   You can find their work at Worldmapper.org.

Originally our plan was to incorporate Worldmapper's morphing map animations (existing and newly created) into the stage work; they generously kept this offer on the table, but it gradually fell away as the process began to focus more on the stories we were gathering. These discussions about the themes of the work opened up different possibilities and attitudes to the project. Starting with detailed discussions about the purpose of maps and mapping, the conversation moved on to the fundamental issue of the purpose of the show.

Some notes we made during that first meeting:

> 'The thing about the number of countries in the world is that it's like the number of bones in the human body. There's about 200, but they are continually breaking in two or fusing back together.'

> 'You can't be emotionally engaged with your subject matter the whole time.'

> 'We are better at abstract thinking than our grandparents – but not as good at planting potatoes. There has been an almost biological change in the audience.'

> 'If someone is happy there is the assumption that they don't need/deserve economic justice.'

At some point in the meeting Danny explained that they see the objective of their work as being to help the viewer to see foreigners – human beings in another country – 'as yourself in another place.' This struck us as a beautiful articulation of our ambitions for this show. We were interested in the stories that people tell about other countries, the stories that stand in for knowing about that country, but we wanted the show to ask, what would it be like to live that story? We were developing a number of texts about geography and mapping, but this conversation was the beginning of our growing understanding that the unique data we had to work with in this show were the stories we were collecting.

Story Map

In order to get ourselves up on our feet and making material, Jorge, Chris and Alex were setting themselves a number of writing, storytelling and text-generating tasks in the making room. One of these was a game that we initially referred to as the *Research Table*, but would go on to call *Story Map*. It started with us trying to create a map

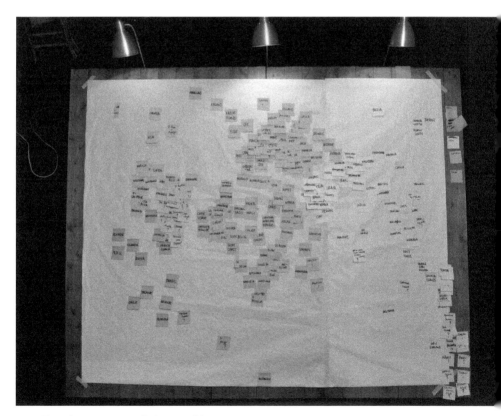

Post-it note map of the world.

of the world, from memory, with post-it notes. We liked how it still looked like the world, even though each country was represented with the same size label.

This developed into an exercise in which we would build the map much more slowly – with a selection of, say, ten countries each, which we would have to place on the map, tell a story about, and then indicate with an icon-like, hand drawn image.

We had been invited to take our story-gathering process to a Forest Fringe Microfestival at The Arches in Glasgow, and we decided to play this new game with the audience. By this point we had settled on using the CIA World Factbook as our definitive country list, partly because it was freely accessible on the internet, and also cheap to buy as a hard copy, and partly because it was so comprehensive, listing contested states and dependent territories. And, as well as listing each country by 'conventional name' (i.e. what the country is called in English), it lists the 'local name' (in short form and long form), too. The name that (the CIA say) the people of each country call the place they live. Over the course of the project, this gave us a country-count of 190 – 192, as those countries did indeed continue to break apart and fuse back together.

Over the course of 6½ hours, across two evenings in Glasgow, we got from Afghanistan to India, about halfway. Collecting and telling stories and generating conversations. We told the stories we already had, and heard lots more. Defining each country with just one story. Defining each story with a two-word title and an icon.

We ran the game later that month as part of work-in-progress showings at the PAZZ Festival in Oldenburg, gathering more stories from a non-UK audience. This live interaction felt like

Chris places the last country on the *Story Map*, Hull 2011. Photo: Hannah Nicklin.

the most fruitful way of collecting stories for the process, and we stopped looking for stories on the internet ourselves. We realised the significance of the show's title, that *What I Heard About the World* had to be made up of stories that other people had told us.

At the end of August 2010, at the start of the autumn making process, we ran *Story Map* again, with Forest Fringe in Edinburgh, this time for 12 hours, which gave us just enough time to complete the map. From this point, *Story Map* grew to become a stand-alone companion piece.[5] In order to be able to corroborate the stories we were putting on the map (we knew this project was not about urban myths), to be able to document the show online, and reach an audience outside

5   For these first Forest Fringe performances, we placed the countries on the map in alphabetical order. But after this we decided that to keep the level of challenge in the mapping task (performed by Chris), we would have to produce the country names on cards, bingo style, in a random order.

of the room of the performance, we introduced a new role, bringing in Hannah Nicklin as live-documenter and dramaturg/researcher. Hannah set up and ran an evolving online archive for us, over five different runs of *Story Map*.

The World Outside the Room

Autumn 2010. Alex, Chris and Jorge were joined more regularly in the process by our co-devisers, director Rachael Walton and designer José Capela, plus Lauren Stanley as documentation and research intern and, for a week of the process, dramaturg Johanna Wall.

Initially we took the giant table of *Story Map* into the devising phase for the theatre version of *What I Heard About the World*, imagining that we would position the stories on it, with the performers working around it, rather like we had at the PAZZ performances.

Making the show was a process of refining. Selecting the stories, from the 180 we had gathered by this point, that meant something to us, individually and as a group. Finding a balance, a selection of stories that painted a picture of the world as we saw it, and that represented the range of stories we had been given. By the end of the first week we felt that the giant map was more of a hinderance, and so we tried working without it, making more room for us as storytellers, and more room for the furniture and props we began to accumulate.

Whilst we struggled to find the frame to hold the stories (a stage that gradually filled with flat daddies, one for every story, was one idea we tried), the stories themselves were finding their own form. We realised that what we were aiming to do was to cast one of us in each story as the protagonist, whose experience the audience were being asked to imagine. We were also keen that each story was told slightly differently, through dialogue, monologue, lecture demonstration, enactment or something else.

A breakthrough came with the story Radio Silence. We knew we wanted this in the show, and had tried several ways of telling it, none of which quite worked. Chris took it away for an hour and came back with the text pretty much exactly as it is in the script you have here. What was key about this section is that the storytelling is its own frame. The radio-on-and-off device brings an element of the experience it describes right into the room with the audience. As we began to build a possible order for the stories we were interested in and had found a way of telling, we began to realise that the frame for our collection of stories was the telling of them. The three performers, talking to each other and the audience, with the stories prepared and rehearsed, but with the collaborative, improvised energy of Story Map.

The precise role of the outside eye/director varies with every collaborative process. In *What I Heard About the World* Rachael instinctively began to look for a physical language for the show – finding different configurations and physical tasks for each story, along with ways of linking them: blood from the Korean Interlude ends up in the fish tank when Jorge washes his hands, followed by salt from the Maldives section to make it the sea for the Hijack story; Alex's blood-soaked overalls from the Massacre shooting become surgical scrubs for the Antarctica story.

Alex and Jorge phoning the Line of the Lord, autumn 2010. Photo: Clive Egginton.

Stories We Didn't Tell

As the process moved forward we began to look at the structure, and what the show was doing, and saying. We were seeking a balance of stories that implicitly and explicitly articulated the political agenda of the show. As that came into focus, we were able to start to rule some stories out.

We knew we needed the stories to be true. We were told a lovely story about the Faroe Islands' all-amateur national football team beating Austria one-nil in a qualifier for Euro '92, because they played at home, barefoot on the beach. The Faroe Islands did indeed beat Austria, but it was in boots on a normal pitch in Sweden.

Alex was a bit in love with the story of the Friendly Floatees, thousands of plastic bath toys spilled from a cargo ship, now being used by oceanographers to track tidal currents as they make their way around the world, some of them apparently endlessly. After much discussion, we decided not to include this story, because the show is about the stories people tell about (people in) other countries.[6]

What we were coming to realise is that we did not want to comment on stories individually. With each story we hoped to ask the audience to imagine what it was like for someone to have lived those events, but not to tell them what to think or feel about that. The juxtaposition of the stories is carefully considered, and the picture of the world that the show describes is deliberately drawn. The show also has a commentary voice, through which some of our choices are acknowledged.

6   This ruling was challenged at a performance of *Story Map* at Hatch in Leicester a couple of years later, when it was pointed out to us that there are so many people on the oceans at any one time, it must be greater than the populations of the smallest countries. Having recently read Rose George's brilliant history of cargo shipping, *Deep Sea and Foreign Going* (2013, also published as *90% Of Everything*), we admit to having more sympathy with this idea now.

From Sheffield to Lisbon

What I Heard About the World opened in the Crucible Theatre's Studio in Sheffield, set in a space that felt very much like a living room. The three performers shared the stories primarily with each other, but also occasionally acknowledged the audience. Unsurprisingly perhaps, this audience awareness and direct address grew gradually throughout the run, but still with a sense of the three storytellers contained in their own domestic space, telling stories about the world beyond its walls. This suited the intimacy of the Crucible's Studio well, in which we were performing diagonally across a square space, with the audience almost on three sides.

What I Heard About the World at the Crucible Studio, Sheffield, autumn 2010.
Photo: Craig Fleming

The space we were transferring to in Lisbon, however, Teatro Maria Matos, has a very different feel – a much wider stage, and a clearly end-on relationship between it and the seating bank. We began rehearsing a new version of the show for Lisbon, whilst we were still running it in Sheffield. The new set felt like we had split the original square space down the middle and opened it like a book to face the audience, placing us very much in the same room as them, and dialling down the fictional environment of the Sheffield living room. The performances embraced this new format, with the balance tipping the other way: the storytelling primarily for the audience, but with the *Story Map* energy of doing this for real, in this moment, allowing for asides and commentary to each other.

Chris warming up on the Portuguese set for *What I Heard About the World*, installed in Theatre de Ville, Paris, 2013.

If the show is about trying to hold an image of the world in your head, and telling stories to describe that image, this second version of the show made it much easier to share that image and those stories with the audience.

When the show returned to the UK for touring in 2011 and 2012, we made a replica of the Portuguese set, recycling elements of the first set, and finding some new objects. The Portuguese set had also introduced more replica objects – a Chinese vase, a cactus and other plastic plants, a stuffed giraffe – and so we found UK versions of these, including taxidermy sculptures of a fox and a stag by Susanna Gent.

What I Heard About the World then toured internationally through to 2015, becoming both companies' most performed show up to that point. For most international gigs we took essential props and asked venues to provide the furniture to create yet another duplicate set.[7] We liked how each of these felt like different versions of the same room, and somehow still familiar to perform in.

---

7   The list of settings included a request for 'a stuffed animal'. We always enjoyed finding out what stuffed (or replica) animal we would be provided with: owl, zebra, stag, another giraffe...

Third Angel and mala voadora present
WHAT I HEARD ABOUT THE WORLD

a co-production with Sheffield Theatres,
Teatro Maria Matos, Lisbon,
and Pazz Performing Arts Festival,
in association with Worldmapper

Devised and performed by
Jorge Andrade, Alexander Kelly & Chris Thorpe

Directed by
Rachael Walton

Designed by
José Capela

Research, video & documentation
Lauren Stanley

Dramaturgical support
Johanna Wall

Online research, documentation & support (*Story Map*)
Hannah Nicklin

Lighting Design
João d'Almeida
James Harrison

Technical Managers
Eduardo Abdala
Craig Davidson

Technical Support
Chris Brown

PR
Jaye Kearney

General Manager (Third Angel)
Hilary Foster

Producers (mala voadora)
Manuel Poças & **Joana Costa Santos**

For Sheffield Theatres:

Artistic Director
Daniel Evans

Chief Executive
Dan Bates

With thanks to:
Danny Dorling, Benjamin Hennig and Anna Barford at Worldmapper; Deborah Pearson, Andy Field and Ellie Dubois and the whole team at Forest Fringe; Christopher Hall and Sheffield Hallam University; Megan Vaughan; Rohan Gunatillake; Mairead Turner; Manuel Reis/ LuxFrágil; Fundação Calouste Gulbenkian; Jardins na Linha; Thomas Kraus and the PAZZ Team; everyone at Sheffield Theatres and Teatro Maria Matos; Susanna Gent for the loan of taxidermy sculptures for the UK tour; and, in particular, the many people who gave us stories for the show.

The original production (in English) premiered at Sheffield Theatres on 14 October 2010. A slightly reworked version (in Portuguese and English) opened at Teatro Maria Matos, Lisbon on 10 November 2010 and toured in Portugal through to December 2010.

This version of the show, with different balances of English and Portuguese depending on the location, toured in the UK, Portugal and internationally through to 2015.

What I Heard About the World was supported by the National Lottery through Arts Council England and Ministerio Cultura, Portugal.

Cast

What I Heard About the World was originally performed by a cast of three: Alex, Chris and Jorge. This script uses the names of the original three male performers, but there is no reason for which the cast needs to be all male in any future performance.

Language

The show toured in a number of different versions as it evolved. This text is the version in English that toured in the UK and internationally in 2012–2015. In the version that was performed in Portugal or Brazil in the same period, Jorge performed the majority of his text in Portuguese, and also delivered one speech, Massacre, that Chris performed in the English version.

The show text is made up of written stories and dialogues and some semi-improvised exchanges. Some text is delivered on mic, when Chris plays guitar, and this is indicated in the text. Generally the performers are talking to the audience, but also talk to each other.

SECTION TITLES *are indicated in bold capitals here, but in performance there was rarely any specific indication that the show had moved on to a 'new bit'.*

Set

The set is a collection of furniture that feels like a cross between a living room and a staff room: metal lockers, tables, banqueting chairs, a sofa, an armchair, bookshelves, a TV and DVD player, fake plants, one or two stuffed animals, a fish tank full of water but no fish. A guitar and stand, a couple of microphones. The original touring production had a Portuguese set and a very similar UK set. International venues often provided the show with a replica version.

HOUSE OPENS

As the audience enter, CHRIS is playing guitar, JORGE is sitting in an armchair and ALEX is asleep on the sofa.

PEOPLE ON FIRE, PEOPLE IN LOVE

CHRIS sings and plays guitar.

CHRIS: Dawn follows night follows day
We'd stopped at this truck stop to eat
We had been taking these pills for days
We needed to find
Somewhere to sleep

The motel had one room to rent
We didn't open the blinds
We lay on the bed and got tired and scared
The cracks in the ceiling
Danced over our eyes

And we could see people on fire
And we could see people in love
The cars on the highway roared by outside
As the World played itself
In a movie above

And everything happens at once
Each life and each moment and fate
Next day we woke and we didn't speak
It's a beautiful world
And we carried its weight

INTRO

ALEX has woken up but doesn't move from the sofa. CHRIS carries on playing the guitar. JORGE picks up a mic and speaks to the audience.

JORGE: When you actually go there you'll understand.

The heat there. It's a different sort of heat. Or the cold. It makes you shiver in a completely new way. The light. They're always going on about the light too.

The people do things differently. They have a different attitude to life. It's really refreshing. They're more open. They'll invite you into their houses. And all the food tastes better. The tomatoes, they really taste of tomatoes, you know? Not of nothing.

There are fruit trees on the street. In the winter, when it snows, everyone has responsibility for the bit of pavement outside their house. Sometimes the old people, they wander off into the bush when they know it's time. You know. To die.

And sometimes the place just smells of shit. You realise you're walking along a pavement that's just concrete slabs balanced over a channel full of human shit. But shit doesn't smell disgusting there, you know? Like it would here. Well it does. It smells disgusting there, too, but it also reminds you that you're alive. That we're all alive.

Did I mention the light?

CHRIS: Yeah.

JORGE: Yeah. I did.

They had a war, a few years ago. You can see it in their faces. It's a kind of quiet dignity. Although they don't like to talk about it. Maybe that's why they drink so much.

But you'll never really go to most of these places, because, how could you? One of the things we have to contend with is there's more and more of the world that we'll know about but never see. But the knowing becomes more necessary because the more we know, the bigger the world gets and the bigger the world gets, the larger the gaps we have to fill in. Just to feel that we're still a part of it. That we know where it is.

DEATH SUIT

During this next, JORGE gathers up some clothes from the hat stand, and crosses to ALEX, whom he dresses in a shirt, tie and jacket. ALEX co-operates, but remains impassive, standing facing the audience.

CHRIS sits at the long table and reads from a foreign newspaper (not English, Portuguese or from the country that the show is being performed in).

CHRIS: When people die in Singapore there is one definitive newspaper of record, *The Straits Times*, and many families will buy an obituary notice in their obit pages. These obits include a photograph and a few lines of text. My grandfather died recently, and as per tradition his widows (he had two wives) and children took out a notice in the paper.

 To do this you have to go to the newspaper's obituary office with a passport photo of the deceased. Most people will have a small headshot left over from their final passport, so that's what has to be used.

 If the man in the photograph is wearing a shirt or a t-shirt they will offer to Photoshop in a 'suit and tie', so they can look smarter in the newspaper. When I was told about the photoshopped 'suit and tie' I looked at the obit pages and realised that most of the dead men there are wearing these fake, superimposed clothes.

 I'd never noticed this before, but once you know this you can see that the newspaper must have at least two 'styles' – so that it doesn't look like everyone who died wore the same suit.

 Also, the suits are not quite perfect, I don't mean in terms of the Photoshop job, which is basically okay, but the ties are slightly off-centre,

CHRIS and JORGE consult briefly to check ALEX's tie is crooked to the correct side.

 I guess this is so they look more realistic; smart, but not perfect.

HIRED MOURNERS

JORGE: Alex, you're dead.

JORGE claps ALEX on the shoulder, making him sit back down on the sofa, and walks away. The rest of this section is semi-improvised, but is basically this:

ALEX: You should cry for me then.

JORGE: What?

ALEX: You should cry for me.

If I'm dead. You should be crying for me.

I'd like to be missed, Jorge. I'd like to be mourned, you know, at my funeral – I'd like a funeral! In fact I'd like you to organise my funeral and I have no false sense of modesty I'd like a BIG funeral with hundreds of people there, all of them really upset. And I'd like everyone there to look back on my life and think about what a great and fulfilled life it was, but more importantly, afterwards, I'd like them to be able to think back to my funeral and think about just how many people there were there, and how popular I must have been and how upset everyone was at my passing. I'd like them to be able to remember weeping and wailing.

JORGE: Good luck with that.

ALEX: I can pay you.

JORGE: Okay.

ALEX: I thought so…

JORGE returns to sit next to ALEX on the sofa. ALEX produces a big stash of fake or Monopoly money from the jacket pocket.

ALEX: Chris, are you ready with the music?

CHRIS: Yes I am... this next story is set in Brazil, but I don't
           know any Brazilian music, so usually what I do at this
           point is I play something Spanish... because usually no
           one can tell the difference.

ALEX: Okay, Jorge – *[paying him some cash]* – I've got some
           euros for you –

JORGE: I used to like those...

ALEX: ... and some Great British Pounds... and I've got some
           rupees, too. Probably a better investment for the future.

           So, what I thought was, if you could introduce an
           undercurrent of moaning and wailing. Just to let all my
           real mourners *[indicates the audience]* know that it's
           okay to show their emotions. It's okay to cry for me.

*JORGE starts to cry. CHRIS starts playing something 'Latin
sounding'.*

           Okay, that's good. If I pay a bit extra you could
           personalise it a bit?

JORGE: OH ALEX ALEX!!

ALEX: Lovely. Now can we get a bit more demonstrative?
           Introduce some choreography? A bit of movement.
           A few changes of height?

*JORGE stands and wails his way centre stage, crying louder. The
guitar gets louder, too.*

           That's good Jorge, but I want tears!

JORGE: What?!

ALEX: Tears! I'm paying for tears!

JORGE runs to the fish tank and throws water over his own face.

Okay that's great. Let's build to a big finish. Look, there goes my coffin! You'll never see me again! If we could have that knee thing – a genuflection? – great…

JORGE collapses, and ALEX throws more money at him.

ALEX: … and stay down, now, stay down, so people have to step over you on their way out.

You do have to be careful, though, Jorge, there are occupational hazards. If you are TOO LOUD, *[guitar quietens]* and the priest cannot be heard, then you can be excommunicated for being too noisy in church.

But overall, I thought that was pretty good. I was quite moved. Thanks.

JORGE picks up the money and is just trying to wangle a bit more out of ALEX with a bit more crying as CHRIS interrupts him –

MALDIVES

Semi-improvised, but very like this:

CHRIS: *[Reading from newspaper.]* 'Islands around the world are sinking…'

No. That's not right.

He abandons the newspaper.

Islands around the world aren't sinking. That's lazy journalism.

The global sea level is rising.

And the lowest lying islands will go first. Places like the Maldives.

ALEX has joined CHRIS at the table, and is taking things out of the metal cabinets and putting them on the table next to him: a one

*litre bottle of water, a funnel, a pint glass, a tea spoon and a carton
or bottle of table salt.*

> Obviously, this is a terrible state of affairs. A lot of people
> are worried about it. I'm worried about it too. In fact when
> Alex asked me how worried I was on a scale of one to
> ten, with one being entirely unconcerned, and ten being
> shitting myself, I said I was about... a nine. Which was
> when Alex explained his idea.

*ALEX is tipping heaped tea spoons of salt into the water bottle,
through the funnel.*

ALEX: I've got this idea that I think will help to alleviate this
          situation. But it's not going to be easy, and I'm going to need
          help. In fact, I'm going to need one very committed volunteer,
          so I was really pleased to hear that Chris was so concerned.

          So, the plan. How many people are there in the world?

A brief discussion, getting answers from audience.

> Well, it's actually about *[up to date figure in billions]*,[1]
> but I'm going to say 7 billion for ease of calculation. Now,
> imagine if every one of those 7 billion people were to
> drink a litre of seawater every day. Let's not worry just
> now about how we get the sea water to all those people.
> That's a logistical issue for later.

CHRIS: Just logistics.

ALEX: Imagine it: you're all drinking a litre of seawater every day,
          that would be 7 billion litres coming out of the sea every day.
          That's 49 billion litres coming out of the sea every week.
          After 2 or 3 months, that's going to have an effect. It's going
          to at least steady the rise. But I'm optimistic, I think it will
          bring some of those beaches back.

1   When we made the show this figure was 6.8 billion, so we rounded the
    number up. As the tour progressed it was alarming how rapidly we had to
    update the number, having added half a billion people to the figure by the
    time the tour ended in 2015.

Of course the issue is that sea water is very salty. In fact, one litre of sea water contains 35 grams of salt. That's seven teaspoons full.

CHRIS: In scientific terms, that's A Fuckload Of Crisps.

ALEX puts the cap back on the bottle of salty water and shakes it up.

ALEX: So it is going to be a challenge. And what we're doing – well, what Chris is doing – is, he's in training, to see how long it takes a normal person to build up their tolerance to drink a litre of sea water a day.

ALEX pours CHRIS half of the saltwater.

CHRIS: So this glass holds about a British pint, or five hundred and sixty-eight millilitres. If we fill it to just below the top, let's say that's five hundred millilitres, or half a litre. What we thought we could do is sell this as: drink half a litre for breakfast, half a litre before bed, like it's Slimfast or something. I'm going to write us a jingle but I haven't got round to it yet.

             So here goes.

Keeps drinking throughout this.

             As with most of the fun things in life, the first thing you need to do is anaesthetize your gag reflex. So we just let a little bit trickle down the back of the throat, like so. Then we can take progressively larger gulps. Now at this point, it still looks like there's a lot to get through. And there is. So it can be a bit daunting. I like to employ some visualisation to get me through it. Basically, every time I take a mouthful, I imagine that a Polar Bear comes back to life.

Drinks.

Vomits into a bucket that is conveniently placed under the table.

He drinks some more.

He vomits, gives up, passes the glass back to ALEX.

ALEX: *[Depending on how CHRIS has done.]* That's not bad/
             That's a bit disappointing... Chris is actually getting a bit
             better at this each day. In the graph of his progress there
             are peaks and troughs, but the overall trajectory is one
             of improvement. To the point now that I'm a bit worried
             about his health. I mean, 35 grams of salt is a lot more
             that your Recommended Daily Allowance isn't it? I'm
             worried that if he is able to do this it could make him
             quite ill, or even kill him.

             But then that makes me think that maybe that's why this
             is such a good idea. If we can get enough people around
             the world to do this, and a significant number of them
             die, then that will reduce the world's population, so that
             will have a positive effect on global warming, and that
             will help those sea levels.

             And of course the bonus will be that anyone who
             dies from drinking a litre of sea water a day will be
             someone who was stupid enough to do it in the first
             place...

CHRIS: It's basically natural selection...

ALEX: And so that makes me think about the people who we
             could force to do this. People in prison – they'd have no
             choice, this is part of your punishment – and what about
             people in hospital, the sick, the elderly...

CHRIS: ... children...

ALEX: And when you think about it, these are the people who
             are the biggest drain on the society's resources aren't
             they? And who put the least back. So now the plan is
             making an economic sense as well as an environmental
             one...

JORGE: *[On mic.]* In fact, we emailed the government of the Maldives with this idea. We thought they could take it to a conference or something. They never replied. And in fact we heard a bit later that they've actually been buying land in Sri Lanka, and India…

CHRIS: Australia…

JORGE: … Australia, as far away from the sea as possible, in the expectation that sometime in the near future they might have to start abandoning their country to the Ocean. Which seems a bit pessimistic. Almost like they've given up already. So. You know. Fuck 'em.

SHORT STORIES 1

ALEX puts a black hood over his own head and sits as if tied to the chair. JORGE joins them at the table, the three of them sat facing the audience.

CHRIS: In Belgium, there's a company called Extreme Outcomes, and what you can do is, if you're a bit bored with your life, you can pay them to provide you with a range of experiences. In one, you're bundled into the back of a car – effectively kidnapped – and tied to a chair for twelve hours while men in ski masks shout at you. And in another you can play the part of a drug smuggler and they chase you. With helicopters.

ALEX: A popular new career choice for young Germans is to become a protestor-for-hire. These protestors rent themselves out using a website – erento.com. If you go to their homepage, you just have to click on the Rent-a-Demonstrator link at the top.

If you're a potential agitator looking for support for your public protest, you might choose, for example, Steffen here…

Indicates CHRIS.

… he's 22 years old, 190cm tall, 'athletic build', shoe size 45.

CHRIS produces a Molotov cocktail from under the table and starts trying to light it.

> For a basic rate, these protestors will turn up and make up the numbers, but at an extra cost they will carry placards and shout slogans. What they won't do, of course, is carry out acts of violence, like throwing a Molotov cocktail, because that would be illegal.

CHRIS blows out the flaming bottle and dumps it in a bin.

JORGE presses speed dial on a phone, holds up the receiver. From the phone we hear voices speaking in French. Projected surtitles translate:

PHONE: *[Female voice.]* After the tone this call will be charged at the rate of 0.34€ per minute, plus an extra connecting fee if you are calling from a mobile phone. For more information contact your operator.

[Music.]

[Male voice.] Hello and welcome to *The Line of The Lord*. This service allows you to confess through self-communion and prayer. It allows you to admit your sins before God and your brothers and to prepare your heart to receive the Holy Grace.

Confession is the exclusive occupation of a priest. You may also confess your sins by putting yourself in the presence of the Lord through self-communion, prayer and faith. *The Line of The Lord*'s vocation is to help you position yourself in the presence of God in order to receive His Grace.

However, in the case of a grave and deadly sin, meaning the sins that have pushed you away from Christ our Lord, it is necessary to confess before a priest, for only he may help you and give you the rite of reconciliation.

[Music.]

To receive instructions for your confession, press 1.

To confess, press 2.

To listen to other people's confessions, press 3.

To return to the first menu, press asterisk.

JORGE hangs up, ALEX removes the bag from his head.

RADIO SILENCE

JORGE switches the radio on.

The three of them sit and listen.

Stillness. Silence.

JORGE: What we're doing is–

Silence.

     We're listening to the radio.

Silence.

     I love this station.

Silence.

     It's run by the Israeli Government. There aren't any news programmes. There's no chart show or Tim Westwood or shipping forecast or lame panel games. Except for the Israeli version of *Just A Minute*. As in *You Have Just A Minute To Get Into The Bomb Shelter Under The House*.

     But hopefully you'll never hear that warning. You'll listen to this station every day of your life and hear nothing more than this.

Silence.

Which means there's nothing to worry about. Except for
the normal day to day worry of living in a tiny country
surrounded by a lot of people who wish you didn't exist.
For various reasons that probably aren't personally your
fault. And almost certainly not your kids' fault. Although
to what extent your government's to blame… well that
depends on who you ask.

At times of crisis, of heightened tension, many Israeli
families tune in to this station. They fall asleep,
nervously I guess, with all the radios on in the house
and this station broadcasting silence. Silence that
will only be broken in the event of an emergency
so imminent that you and your family have to take
immediate action.

And broadcasting silence is actually what it does. It's
not like the station is off, and then suddenly takes over
its set frequency when something dire and threatening
unfolds.

The station actually, actively, broadcasts every minute
of every day. And unless there's something incredibly
urgent to say, what it broadcasts is this.

Silence.

Which is very different to –

JORGE switches the radio off.

Silence.

This.

Because this –

He switches the radio on.

Silence.

Is active. It's saying we're ready. We're alert. All the inward and outward looking eyes of the state security apparatus are open and synced and attuned to the minutest variations in the global political and military flux within which our country has carved out a precarious right to exist. We might be surrounded by potential nuclear weapons states that say they want to vaporize us. We might have within the wider borders of our own country a significant number of pissed-off people crowded into some of the most densely populated, under-resourced areas on Earth, a situation which we don't exactly do much to alleviate. By smiting them from time to time with disproportionate force. These things are true, but the fact that you're hearing this –

Silence.

– right now, means that all these things are currently under control.

Whereas this –

He switches the radio off.

Silence.

This just means your radio's broken. Or you need to replace the batteries. Because this isn't the sound of silence being broadcast. It's the sound of no signal being received. It's the sound of nothing at all. So you won't know if this –

Switches the radio on.

Silence.

– has stopped, and been replaced by an announcement. And the moment you realise that you were listening to this –

Radio off.

Silence.

> – after all, the rockets will already be falling. Or you'll
> be choking while you try to get the gas masks onto your
> kids' faces.
>
> What I'm saying is, at times of crisis in Israel, your
> ability to be forewarned enough to survive... Well. It
> could basically rest on being able to tell the difference
> between this –

Radio off.

Silence.

> And –

Radio on.

Silence.

> This.
>
> I think I'll leave it running. Just in case.

CHRIS goes to the mic and picks up the guitar, starts playing.

ALEX pours whisky for himself and JORGE. They drink.

CHRIS: Ah. None of us have ever been to Israel. That's kind of
the point. Most of the stories, the stories we carry in our
heads at least, are about places we've never been to. But
it's integral, to most of us at least, to our sense of identity
to have that sense of place. So we bolt those stories
together to give the illusion of a solid framework. They
are just stories, though. Even the most complicated of
them can only really stand in for complexity.

              That said, all of the stories are true.

*ALEX gets a drawing pad and marker pen from the cupboard,
starts drawing.*

There is a radio station in Israel, for example, that broadcasts silence until it's needed. That is a fact. Israeli families do fall asleep listening to it. That is also a fact.

But we're acutely aware there's more than one side to that particular story.

The Palestinian-Israeli conflict is the one conflict, as a good liberal, that it's kind of compulsory to have an opinion on. If only so you've got something to talk about at parties.

And it almost felt as if we were letting the Israeli family in the story off too lightly if we didn't also imagine a Palestinian family. The Palestinian family, they're maybe only two or three miles down the road from the Israeli family. And they haven't got electricity or a radio station to warn them of anything. They're in their cellar. And they're looking at each other by candle-light.

[Getting gradually more upset.] And they're thinking, is today the day that the bulldozers are going to come and demolish our house? Or they're looking at their eldest daughter – she's maybe only thirteen – and thinking, tomorrow, when she goes to school,

ALEX shows JORGE, and the audience, a picture of a donkey. Then he carries on, clearly drawing over the donkey.

... or she goes out to the market, will tomorrow be the day that she catches a sniper's bullet and we never see her again?

[Brightening up.] We did get two stories for the Palestinian Territories though. One was about a guy trying to smuggle a Snow White costume into the West Bank. It turned out okay. And the other one – the other one was about Gaza Zoo:

ALEX: In Gaza Zoo, they don't have any zebras.

They do have a lot of donkeys though.

So what they do is: they paint the donkeys black and white.

He shows the donkey, now with stripes drawn down it.

FLAT DADDY

JORGE reveals a life-size, free-standing drawing of himself in army fatigues.

ALEX: This is Bryan. Flat Bryan, I call him.

Flat Bryan is part of an official US Government programme called Flat Daddies.

When American Servicemen (and women) go overseas, to fight in, Afghanistan, say, the National Guard sends a life-size, photographic cut-out of them to keep their families company.

And these flat dads get taken out on trips to the shopping mall, and to events at schools and to family parties... but mainly they stay at home, they stand in the living room, or in the children's bedrooms. And the kids talk to them and include them in their games. And in fact the children are becoming increasingly attached to these Flat Daddies.

JORGE has picked up the phone and is listening.

JORGE: To the point where, now, when Round Bryan phones up from Afghanistan to speak to his wife, Debbie, and his little girl, Sarah... oh...

He hangs up.

Sarah won't speak to him, because she says her real dad is already home.

JOURNEY ONE

CHRIS is still on mic, and his guitar playing gets louder, so he has to shout over it. During this speech JORGE is looking for something on stage – on the shelves, in the cabinets, in ALEX's pockets. He ends up sitting on the sofa. ALEX stays at the table writing on index cards and drinking whisky.

CHRIS: So we would have taken Singapore Airlines flight SQ474 from Changi airport to Dubai, then Emirates to Brazil to see the hired mourners. That's an Emirates flight. EK2717 to Rio de Janeiro. By now we've already travelled over 13,000 miles – that's over halfway round the world. Then it's an internal flight – but don't worry, although it's in South America it's between two major cities so it's fairly safe. Brasilia Air to Sao Paolo. Then back across the Atlantic with Emirates EK 2340 to Dubai again. Then it's the Maldives so another Emirates flight to Male – that's not Mali the African country, it's Male the capital of the Maldives. Then back again to Dubai. Then to get to Israel, weirdly the best thing to do is to fly to Egypt on Egypt Air and then because Egypt and Israel are getting on okay at the moment you can take El Al to Ben Gurion Airport. Probably not worth trying to get the papers to get into the Palestinian Territories so now it's American Airlines AA784 straight to JFK. By this time we're over thirty thousand miles – much more than a circumnavigation of the world. Then it's a short commuter hop north to Buffalo, New York to see Debbie, Sarah and Flat Bryan. We've caught up with ourselves now so it's Air France to Paris Charles de Gaulle and then LOT Airways, that's the Polish national airline, to Warsaw, where the airport's named after Frédéric Chopin, but don't get excited – it's still a fucking airport. Then it's another LOT flight about 1,300 miles southeast to the Caucasus – to Tblisi, the capital of Georgia. Well over 40,000 miles now. And in Tblisi we do something we haven't done before. We get on a bus heading west. And on the bus. On the bus. On the...

NATASHAS

CHRIS: On a bus, travelling west between Georgia and
           Turkey right now, a young woman sits by the window,
           watching the landscape change from the familiar to
           the new.

He hangs up the guitar and sits next to JORGE on the sofa.

           She is beautiful.

JORGE smiles.

           She is one of twelve beautiful young Georgian women
           on this bus. They don't know each other – they're spread
           out among the families and the middle-aged and the
           students and the poor.

*ALEX finishes up his writing, and pays attention to the story, still
drinking whisky.*

CHRIS produces JORGE's real passport from his pocket.

           When the bus reaches the Turkish border, the young
           women will show their passports, and smile. The border
           police will check the faces in the photographs carefully.
           Some of the photographs will be recent but a few will be
           years old. The border police will look from photographs
           to faces especially carefully in these cases. Because what
           they're trying to see in the photograph of a girl of eleven
           or twelve is the made-up face of a woman of eighteen or
           twenty. They will ask the women their dates of birth and
           their names, which are printed in neat Latinate lettering
           below the photograph.

           The young Georgian woman will have names like:

*JORGE lists their names. CHRIS tries to keep up with translations
of them, not entirely successfully:*

JORGE: Bedisa.

CHRIS: It's fate.

JORGE: Dedismedi.

CHRIS: Mother's hope.

JORGE: Chiora.

CHRIS: Bird.

JORGE: Endzela.

CHRIS: Snowdrop.

JORGE: Gogutsa.

CHRIS: Little girl.

JORGE: Gvantsa.

CHRIS: Crazy/wild...

JORGE: Irema.

CHRIS: Deer.

JORGE: Vardo.

CHRIS: Rose.

JORGE: Tsitsia.

CHRIS: Heavenly.

JORGE: Thinathini.

CHRIS: Sunbeam.

JORGE: Xatia.

CHRIS: Like an icon or painting.

JORGE: Pikria.

CHRIS: Thinker.

JORGE: Pepela.

CHRIS: Butterfly.

JORGE: Phirimthvarisa.

CHRIS: The mouth of the moon.

Then the bus will drive over the border, on into Turkey, towards Europe. And a funny thing will happen to these young Georgian women. Every single one of them will disappear.

The women who get off the bus at the terminal will look the same. They'll smoke the same brand of cigarettes, and check their make-up in mirrors held too close to their faces because the light is bad.

But all of the beautiful young women who get off the bus will be called Natasha. And as well as sharing a name, they'll also share a date of birth. Because Natasha – and it's not lost on these Georgian women that Natasha is a Russian name – means 'Born on Christmas Day'.

ALEX joins them on the sofa, sitting next to JORGE.

From the border town – it's usually a town called Sarpi – the line of Natashas will split and curve across the map. If you looked at it from above, it'd be like the traces of a firework. They're travelling from East to West – the same route that goods have always taken. Men are waiting across Turkey, the Balkans, Eastern and Western Europe, Scandinavia.

JORGE reaches into ALEX's jacket pocket and produces a wedge of fake bank notes.

> They're going to pick up Natashas at train stations,
> in car parks, and take them to anonymous looking
> buildings in the suburbs or walk-up flats in city centres
> where some of the Natashas might be lucky. But most of
> them will be very unlucky indeed. They'll all learn some
> of the local language though – they'll learn to say words
> like –

JORGE: *[Counting the money.]* Euros. Pounds. Dollars. Kuna. Dinars. Kroner. Francs. Rubles. Liras...

And they'll learn to introduce themselves–

JORGE: Hi, my name is Natasha...

ALEX: Hello, Natasha!

JORGE: Ich bin Natasha,
minya zavoot Natasha,
jam sam Natasha,
chamo-me Natasha,
me lhamo Natasha,
Je m'appelle Natasha.

They kiss. CHRIS fires a party cannon over the sofa.

IRANIAN MARRIAGE

The three of them are still sprawled on the sofa.

JORGE: In Iran, sex before marriage is illegal. But, it's possible
to get married – officially, legally married – for a limited
amount of time – usually for twenty-four hours, or even
for a week. This is great, as it allows you to have sex
with your boyfriend or girlfriend without getting into
trouble.

CHRIS extricates himself, leaving JORGE and ALEX entwined on the sofa, and crosses to the armchair.

CHRIS: Of course this doesn't work if you're gay, though. If you're gay and you try this – not just in Iran but in a lot of places – you'll be arrested. Then you'll be dragged through the streets to a public place, probably a square, and there'll be one of those trucks. You know the ones with the arm on the back for towing cars? And you'll be made to stand of the back of the truck, and they'll put a rope around the arm and put the other end around your neck, and then they'll kick you off the back of the truck and your neck will break. Or actually you'll probably asphyxiate, which is slower.

It's not all bad news though. Because people will film all that on their mobile phones, and then put it on the internet.

CHRIS fires a party cannon over the armchair.

JORGE and ALEX slowly take their arms from around each other. They exchange a look.

DATA KID

ALEX: My name's Kim. I'm 41. *[To JORGE.]* You're my wife –

JORGE: My name is Anna. I'm 26.

ALEX: Our little girl, she's called –

They indicate CHRIS.

JORGE: She's called Aecha.

ALEX: She's three months old, and we're –

JORGE: We're just so incredibly proud of her.

ALEX: Every day with her is like a whole new adventure.

JORGE: And she's so good.

ALEX: She never cries.

JORGE: And she always sleeps through.

ALEX: And it's such a joy to watch her learn things. To pick up experience.

JORGE: We feed her. Or rather –

ALEX: We just guide her towards the food, and she feeds herself, which at three months is pretty amazing.

JORGE: She's incredibly emotionally responsive.

ALEX: She takes real pleasure in things, and seeing her take pleasure in things, it –

JORGE: It brings us closer together...

A moment together.

            And she can walk already.

ALEX: She can run, in fact.

JORGE: It's so wonderful to see her running through the forests and climbing up the waterfalls.

ALEX: And we think, in a couple of weeks, when she's gained enough experience points, she'll be able to start flying.

JORGE: We're going to teach her.

ALEX: Which will make it so much easier getting from one place to another.

JORGE: And then we're going to upgrade her armour.

ALEX: And increase her magical powers.

JORGE: Like healing, and talking to animals, and self-defence.

ALEX: Just self-defence. We want our child to be able to protect herself. We don't want her to be violent, do we?

JORGE: Even a world as wonderful as the one she lives in can be dangerous sometimes.

ALEX: We're looking forward to watching her grow and learn. We hope she never stops doing that. And we hope she never stops loving us, either.

JORGE: I never –

ALEX: It's okay. You can say it.

JORGE: I never thought I'd love anyone so much as I love her.

ALEX: We love her so much we're saving our money.

JORGE: Which is hard, because with Aecha, it's difficult for us to work at the moment. We've been spending every minute we can with her because it makes us feel so alive to watch her grow.

ALEX: To come along with her.

JORGE: On her adventures.

ALEX: So we're saving our money to buy a computer.

JORGE: One that will be ours. For the apartment.

ALEX: So we can be with her 24 hours a day.

JORGE: Instead of having to leave her alone overnight.

ALEX: It breaks our heart to leave her, but we have to, because the internet café closes.

JORGE: That's our goal. Currently. As a couple.

ALEX: We don't want anything to get in the way of that.

JORGE: So we were surprised.

ALEX: We were surprised… when they told us about the other baby.

JORGE: We really didn't know anything about it.

ALEX: Which was strange, because they said it had been living in our apartment.

JORGE: But neither of us can remember seeing it before.

ALEX: Was it a boy or a girl?

JORGE: I think it was a little girl.

ALEX: … just a few months old, they said.

JORGE: But we never heard it.

ALEX: We never heard it cry or anything.

JORGE: You would have thought a baby that age would have cried.

ALEX: It must have been really thin.

JORGE: The poor thing must have been really hungry.

ALEX: When they told us about it, it just made us more relieved that we'd looked after Aecha properly.

JORGE: Some people just don't deserve to have children.

ALEX: It's not our fault, of course, but we don't get to spend as much time with Aecha these days.

JORGE: Not nearly as much as we'd want to.

ALEX: It's hard, when you're moving from place to place.

JORGE: We didn't know what to do.

ALEX: When they took the baby away, the one that someone left in our apartment, when they took it to the hospital, where it died, they said they had to ask us some questions.

JORGE: But we thought that would take up too much time. Time we could be spending with our daughter.

ALEX: So we thought it would be best to go somewhere else. Maybe move around for a while. After all, there are internet cafés everywhere.

JORGE: We just want to be with our little girl.

KOREAN INTERLUDE

CHRIS: [On mic, with guitar.] So that was a story from Korea, or more specifically from South Korea.

           The Korean Peninsula is obviously divided into two countries. South Korea and North Korea.

           But it wasn't the only story we heard about Korea. Or more accurately, both Koreas.

           And we heard more stories about the two Koreas than for any other area of the world.

           And we thought. Well, that's probably not a coincidence. And also that probably means we should recognise that by having some sort of... Korean interlude. So this – what's about to happen here – is the Korean Interlude.

JORGE and ALEX have crossed the stage, collected some props from the cabinets and sat together at the end of the table. ALEX starts to draw on JORGE's palm.

> The thing about Korea is, it's very far away. I mean it's not far away if you live in Japan, but it's a long way from here, and we don't know that much about it. So that makes the idea of Korea really useful. Because we all need to roll our eyes sometimes, don't we, at the weirdness of the world? And if we can hear a story, then roll our eyes and go – 'only in Korea eh?' – and that makes us feel better about the weirdness, well that's brilliant. So Korea's like a repository for all the crazy shit that goes on. South Korea is a country made up entirely of neon, and run by robots – actual robots. And North Korea can't feed its population. But they do have nuclear weapons. And they're not that interested in talking to us, so they could be up to literally anything in there.
>
> Korea's like our safety valve for oddness. If you were to ask a random selection of British people to sum up Korea in three words, most of them would probably say... 'They eat dogs.'
>
> The thing is, that's not even true. Korean people, in the main, they don't really eat dogs. It's kind of a myth. Or to put it another way, they only eat dogs in the same circumstances that you or I would. Like if they were really fucking hungry.

JORGE screams. ALEX is now drawing on his palm with fake blood.

> Another useful thing about the two Koreas is that we see them as very different in their weirdness.

JORGE screams.

> South Korea, as we've seen, is where people love their virtual kids so much they leave their real ones to starve.

JORGE screams.

> And North Korea's like the fourteen-year-old boy of the international community – doesn't want to communicate, probably doesn't eat very well. Never leaves the house.

JORGE screams.

> So in the Korean interlude we thought we'd get all that out of the way.

JORGE crosses the stage, showing the audience his bleeding palm.

> In South Korea, there is a pervasive belief that if you physically alter the lines on the palm of your hand, you actually alter your future. And there are plastic surgeons willing to do this for money. Young Korean people get their palm read, compare the predictions they get to the future they want for themselves, and then have the lines on their palms lengthened or shortened or deepened. With scalpels.

JORGE washes the blood from his hands in the fish tank.

ALEX starts demonstrating the following with hand-drawn, 2D wigs.

> And in North Korea there are only five state-sanctioned haircuts for men. And if you deviate too much from these haircuts, you can be named and shamed on national TV in a candid camera show called – *Let's All Trim Our Hair For The Glory Of The Socialist Revolution.*
>
> So the Korean interlude of the show is basically here to do what the idea of Korea does in daily life. It's there to make us all feel that little bit more normal.

ALEX crosses the stage and adds a load of salt to the fish tank.

JORGE washes his hands again, and screams.

JOURNEY TWO

ALEX flies a hand-drawn plane around the stage. JORGE dries his hands, crosses to the table, gets a drink, tidies up the blood.

CHRIS: *[On mic, loud guitar.]* So moving on we fly from Istanbul to Tehran on Turkish Airlines. Then it's north to Moscow on Aeroflot to get KAL – Korean Airlines flight KAL458 the length of Siberia direct to Seoul. In Seoul we only have one option, that's Air Koryo, the North Korean Airline. Don't worry, they've never crashed. So it's Air Koryo to Pyongyang, then back to Seoul. Then we're moving on again. Seoul to Dubai on Emirates. Then Alitalia to Milan. Then a bigger Alitalia plane south to Addis Ababa in Ethiopia. Then in Addis Ababa we get on an Ethiopian Airlines plane south to Nairobi. But about half an hour after take-off, something happens...

HIJACK

ALEX: There are three hijackers in the cockpit of an Ethiopian Airlines Boeing 767-260ER. Flight number 961, Addis Ababa to Nairobi. And we are the hijackers. And we die on 23rd November 1996, along with 122 other people, because we made some assumptions about the way airlines operate that were fundamentally... wrong.

        You could say, in fact, that we were victims of the airline industry's relentless drive towards efficiency. How did we get it so wrong?

JORGE: Como?

CHRIS: I have no idea...

ALEX lands the plane on the table and then produces the index cards he was writing earlier.

ALEX: Chris, you are an airline executive. This is in your office.

Jorge, you and I are students doing a report on 'How the airline industry operates'. Chris, you've agreed to meet us because we're at school with your daughter. Is that enough to go on?

CHRIS: What's my name?

ALEX: Mr Dennehy. But you've told us we can call you Mark.

CHRIS: Er, how old am I?

ALEX: You're 47 years old.

You come from Tampa, Florida.

You did a business degree at UCLA. You wake up every morning and can't really understand how you got here, and in about ten years you'll drink enough to kill yourself. Does that help?

CHRIS: Yeah. Thanks. That's very detailed.

ALEX: We're girls. Attractive, 17-year-old girls. Jorge is the cheerleader type and I'm more of a grungy, quiet one. Very shy, but very pretty under the fringe.

CHRIS: *[Improvised each performance, something like:]* You're the one who I, well Mr Dennehy, will fantasise about tonight...

ALEX: You're getting a bit too into this now... So we're about halfway through the interview, and Jorge, you say this:

Hands JORGE a card.

JORGE: So why don't you fill the planes up with fuel for every trip, Mr Dennehy?

ALEX: Chris, you say:

Hands CHRIS and JORGE cards line by line:

CHRIS: Call me Mark.

JORGE: Mark.

CHRIS: That's a very good question, Mandie.

ALEX: Your name's Mandie, by the way, Jorge. Spelled with an 'ie', and you sign it with a little heart over the 'i'.

Hands CHRIS two more cards:

CHRIS: Well, Mandie, the reason we don't fill up the planes with fuel for every flight is that the heavier the aircraft is, the more fuel it needs to burn to get it off the ground and to keep it flying. So we calculate the amount of fuel we put in the plane carefully for every trip, and only put in the fuel the plane needs to make the trip, plus a percentage as a contingency in case something doesn't go according to plan, so the plane can divert to an alternate airport, for example. If we put in excess fuel, the unburned fuel would simply constitute more weight that the aircraft had to burn more fuel to lift off the ground, thereby making the whole process of flight much more inefficient and environmentally damaging.

ALEX: You see? Now, if the three hijackers had heard that, they might still be alive today. Along with 122 other people.

            Now we're the hijackers again.

Continues flying the carboard plane around the stage.

            We broke into the cockpit with a fire axe we'd taken from an emergency box on the wall, and a bottle of whisky wrapped in a t-shirt that the pilot thought was a bomb because we told him:

CHRIS
& JORGE: This is a bomb!

ALEX: We broke into the cockpit and demanded to be taken to
           Australia. We had chosen Australia because we read
           in the inflight magazine that the Boeing 767 can fly
           from Ethiopia to Australia. But as we've just heard, just
           because a plane can fly that distance, that doesn't mean
           it is carrying enough fuel to do so.

ALEX climbs across the sofa and onto the table.

           We didn't know that, and once we had got to Australia
           our plan was to apply for political asylum.

CHRIS: Which I guess would have been our second big mistake
           because we'd be turning up in Australia with a planeload
           of people who didn't really want to be there. So I'm
           saying I doubt they'd have looked too kindly on our
           asylum application.

ALEX: Of course, which the pilot tried to point out to us, and he
           just kept flying south.

           But we looked out of the window and we could see we
           were still within sight of the east African coast, so we
           knew something was up,

Off the table, via the armchair.

           so we told the pilot

CHRIS
& JORGE: Left! Turn left!

ALEX: Which he did, unbeknownst to us, setting a course for
           the small island nation of the Comoros.

*He turns the plane and flies it across the front of the stage, slowly
losing altitude as it goes.*

           He thought that he could probably make it to land there,
           and, given our rather shaky grasp of geography, maybe

even persuade us that we were actually landing in Australia, and get us the fuck off his plane.

It was a good plan, that was actually working, up to the inevitable moment when the plane ran out of fuel.

Arrives at the fish tank.

The left wingtip touched the surface of the ocean first, tearing off the port engine. The plane turned over, the wings separated from the body and the fuselage landed upside-down in the shallow coastal waters, just a few hundred metres from the beach.

Drops the plane into the fish tank.

The pilot and the co-pilot survived, along with about 50 other people.

The pilot had been hijacked twice before. After this one, they gave him a medal.

A pause.

SHORT STORIES 2

(Semi-improvised; ALEX's stories are different each night; in the English version, JORGE tells a story in Portuguese, without surtitles; in Portugal, he remains silent.)

CHRIS: In Australia, 80% of the speaking parts for male Aboriginal characters in film and on TV are played by the same actor.

In the original production, ALEX chose different stories each night from the research.

ALEX: *[For example.]* In China, they have a growing problem with air pollution. And it has got so bad recently that one enterprising company has made a fortune by selling cans of fresh air. It has turned out to be so popular they now do a range of flavours. Last year's best sellers were *Pristine Tibet* and *Post-Industrial Taiwan*.

JORGE tells a story in Portuguese, with no surtitles. If anyone in the audience speaks Portuguese, it becomes a conversation with them. CHRIS and ALEX sit and wait. Something like this:

JORGE: A Alemanha é o país da Europa – é o país da Europa não, é o país do mundo – onde existe uma maior percentagem de pessoas que vive sozinha. E as pessoas vivem sozinhas não porque se vejam obrigadas a isso ou porque… porque se divorciaram ou porque… porque são viúvas mas por…

Há aqui alguém que perceba português?

Some audience members respond. JORGE speaks to them.

Ah, então, ficaram os três juntos! Que coincidência!

Já se tinham falado lá fora? Pois, olha…

Eu já tinha visto no início que tinham ficado os três juntos. Bom, é a Ivanie, é… e no meio, eu há bocado acabei por… como? Vítor, eu há bocado não tinha perguntado o teu nome.

Returning to the story:

Bom, então a história era… é de… quem nos contou esta história foi uma senhora de cerca de quarenta anos, que ela vivia sozinha, ela tinha um trabalho, era bastante bem-sucedida no seu trabalho, e ela tinha uns CD's com barulhos domésticos para quando ela chegava a casa para se sentir acompanhada. Ela apesar de ser por iniciativa própria que vivia sozinha, ela não gostava de viver sozinha, então o som… eu costumo fazer isto, isto faz algum sentido quando ninguém me está a perceber, agora assim… vamos lá ver se vocês conseguem adivinhar qual era o som que ela punha quando chegava a casa. Que era um… Ela punha na sala ao lado. Que era:

JORGE makes a low humming noise.

O quê, que som é este?

Somebody answers from the audience.

Sim!

Mas há outros sons. Há sons tipo de pessoas a falar baixinho na sala ao lado ou a lavarem a louça, ou alguém a limpar o pó com os bibelots a tocarem uns nos outros e eventualmente um cai, tudo isto para as pessoas não se sentirem tão sozinhas. O que não é o meu caso hoje porque estão aqui três pessoas, normalmente estou eu a falar sozinho e esta gente ninguém me compreende nada não é? Mas olha...

CHRIS: In Greenland there obviously aren't very many people. So if you get sent to prison, they have to let you out every day to do whatever your normal job is. But for the length of your sentence, everyone ignores you.

ALEX: *[For example.]* In India they have gangs of criminal monkeys. Little monkeys who come into towns and villages, break into people's houses, steal food, and then get away easily because they can climb really quickly and not be caught. They've got so cocky that now they even mug people in the street. So the people of India knew they had to find specialist help, help that was just as fast, just as good at climbing. So they've trained up some new police officers: bigger monkeys.

MASSACRE

CHRIS returns to the mic and guitar.

During this JORGE and ALEX position a chair to the side and front of the stage, then methodically cover the chair and much of the stage in large sheets of polythene.

CHRIS: So.

Obviously, the world's a place where human beings do
stuff. And if you think the world's a place where human
beings do stuff, you can't avoid the fact that quite a lot
of the stuff that human beings do is about killing each
other. Or having arguments that spread and spill over
into violence.

I mean, it'd be stupid not to acknowledge that. We don't
think the world is a terrible place. It's not all about
human misery. But there has to be some recognition that
the odd massacre takes place. That sometimes one group
of people will isolate and kill another group of people
for a host of reasons so socially and historically complex
that we could write a book just about that one incident
and its origins, but also for the very simple reason that
at that moment in that particular place, they just want to.

So we need a massacre. I guess to stand in for all
massacres, because once you start making an atrocity
list where do you stop.

Basically, we had to choose a massacre. But the criteria
by which something is judged to be a massacre are
pretty wide. So the variety and scale of incidents to
choose from is huge.

You don't want something where too few people died.
They seem to be pretty good at this kind of killing in
Northern Ireland and the US. A guy shoots maybe three
people dead in a betting shop or a sorting office in 'x'-
town and suddenly that's the 'x'-town massacre. I mean
to me, that's a tragedy. An act of terrorism or madness,
yes. But a massacre in which fewer people have died
than in a common or garden everyday kind of accident
– not a plane crash or a nuclear meltdown or something,
but the prosaic, everyday kind of accident isn't really
a massacre. Not really the kind of massacre we'd want
anyway.

I'm playing a bit of music right now, you might have
noticed. This is kind of... well I know it's kind of lame.

But it's building atmosphere. It's our Massacre Music.

So we need something substantial. If we need a single incident to stand in for the worst political excesses of human nature we probably need to set some kind of lower limit to the number of people killed. And an upper limit.

Maybe, we were thinking, not less than fifty people and not more than... a thousand, say. Now a thousand people seems like a weirdly low upper limit to set. But this is where the definition of a massacre comes in. It's useful, in a way, that we get to choose our own parameters. You could argue that the Stalinist purges or the Holocaust were massacres, obviously. And they did contain massacres. Part of the fabric of their mind-boggling numbers is obviously constructed from massacres. Specific incidents in which a whole bunch of people were killed at the same time. But these things, like most mass killings, took place over an extended period of time. The massacre we're looking for, we felt, had to be an incident that wasn't a constituent part of a wider thing. Obviously, all massacres are this to some extent. Srebrenica was part of the war in Bosnia for example. But it has its own identity as a massacre. People who know nothing about the war itself have at least heard of it even if they couldn't tell you who was killing who. Srebrenica's a good candidate for our massacre, but there's something weirdly extended about its timeline when you look at it carefully. Srebrenica is kind of ragged around the edges. It started slowly, peaked after a day or so and petered out as Muslim men and boys were mopped up over the following days. Srebrenica's got the profile, but it hasn't got the edges. Our massacre, we thought, it needs to have happened in a single day. A discrete unit of time. Over a single night, tops. Done by sunrise, or better still within a whole morning.

JORGE and ALEX have completed the polythene sheeting. JORGE dresses ALEX in protective white overalls, goggles, gloves, shoe covers and a mask.

Thing is, it also needs to be non-iconic. By which we mean non-historical. So massacres that are remembered, here at least, for their political impact, or the heroic status of those who were massacred, aren't right, because we don't think about the dead and the horror and disposing of the bodies, but we think more about their effect on the voting system, like Peterloo in Manchester, where I'm from. But at Peterloo there were less than twenty killed so it's more of an incident, really.

And it's probably better, or it feels better, to go for a massacre in which most of the people killed, if not all, were shot. Shot with bullets fired out of guns. Probably by people in uniform. One where the people shooting were wearing uniforms and the people being shot weren't. That just feels right. It feels like something with a clear moral demarcation. It doesn't have the 'these things happen in a war' ambiguity of a bunch of disarmed soldiers being machine-gunned by the other side, and it doesn't have the kind of low-fi, DIY feel of ten thousand people herded into a cathedral and chopped up with machetes, which probably happened either a long time ago, and so the horror has faded, or quite recently and in Africa, so we're less likely to give a shit about it. And also a massacre essentially carried out with farming implements, you think, or at least I do, 'why didn't they just run away?' And that just distracts you from thinking about it.

And finally, we thought it'd be good to have a massacre with its own theme song. Because this –

He stops playing guitar.

– is just a bit dramatic. It's a bit self-conscious. A bit crap.

ALEX crosses the stage to sit in position.

JORGE gets out four pump-action water guns out of the cabinet and sets them on the table.

CHRIS: *[Off mic now.]* So, the Santa Cruz massacre, which we're using to be our massacre to stand in for all the others in the world, took place in Dili, the capital of East Timor, which is now a country but back then was part of Indonesia, which was kind of the point of why the massacre happened, because the people who got killed were marching peacefully in order to demand the independence that East Timor achieved some years later – happened, conveniently for the people who had to clear up I guess, in the Santa Cruz cemetery in 1991. It was ordered by General Wiranto of the Indonesian Army. Interestingly, General Wiranto wasn't there though. He wasn't actually on the ground as his troops were slaughtering the unarmed independence protesters. He was in Jakarta. He gave the order for the massacre to happen and then while it was taking place he was actually filmed in his favourite karaoke bar, belting out a few of his favourite songs.

CHRIS turns the TV monitor on and fires up the DVD player. He sings a karaoke version of 'Feelings' by Morris Albert.

Throughout this JORGE shoots ALEX repeatedly with fake blood from the water pistols.

Eventually, ALEX stops JORGE, and takes of his goggles and mask. He crosses to CHRIS and switches the karaoke off. CHRIS stops singing.

ANTARCTICA

ALEX: After the massacre they cleared away the bodies.

And after they had cleared away the bodies

and after the twelve beautiful women got off the bus and disappeared

and the American soldier came home and tried to convince his little girl he was her real dad and the Korean guy got a proper revolutionary haircut

and the couple came home to their silent flat with no baby crying in it

and the Brazilian woman had cried herself hoarse at the stranger's funeral

and the plane-crash survivors had dragged themselves out of the water and onto the beach

and the entire population of the Maldives had been moved above the waterline

and after the Palestinian kid said, 'Mummy, why is that Zebra melting in the rain?'

After all these things had happened. Something else happened, of course. This time in Antarctica. Which isn't actually a country.

And a woman sitting in Antarctica knew she was going to become a story. Because the woman was determined not to die.

They find their positions, ALEX and JORGE either side of the stage, CHRIS at the table, near the centre. They do not act out or mime any of the medical procedure in the following.

JORGE: I know we've been over this.

ALEX: Yes, we've been over this –

CHRIS: It's cold at the bottom of the world, and at this time of year, the darkness gets longer every day and the weather is getting worse. There won't be any planes for a month or two. She misses her kids.

JORGE: Are you sure –

ALEX: Yes. I'm sure.

CHRIS: If she waits, there's a chance that there'll be a break in the weather, and a supply plane will be able to make its way in to land on the ice runway. Of course there's every chance that the weather's not going to break for weeks, in which case she's missed out on two weeks' worth of treatment, waiting, while the tumour she's found grows bigger. Establishes itself more deeply in her body.

ALEX: Are we going to do this, or what?

JORGE: Relax.

ALEX: I am relaxed.

CHRIS: These two women are just under ten thousand miles apart.

JORGE: Have you marked the incision point?

ALEX: I have.

CHRIS: They are speaking via video-link. One can see what the other is looking at on a monitor, which at the moment is a close-up of her own hands, holding a scalpel and a swab, and the nipple and the underside of her left breast.

ALEX: [Mumbles to self.]

JORGE: Say again.

ALEX: Sorry. I said, 'I'm ready.'

CHRIS: She is the only trained medical professional on the entire base, and she is operating on herself.

JORGE: How does that feel?

ALEX: Fine. I mean. Yeah, fine: I can't feel anything.

JORGE: It's looking good. Now hold the edges of the incision apart.

CHRIS: Slowly working through the other doctor's instructions, she slices into her own body.

JORGE: Now cut carefully around the growth.

ALEX: I can see it. It's coming free.

CHRIS: The world is a slightly squashed sphere, bulging out around the equator, 25,000 miles in diameter, and she is right at the bottom of it.

JORGE: Are you ready to close up now?

CHRIS: Approximately 30% of its surface area is land. More than seven billion people live on that land, and almost none of them are anywhere near her right now.

ALEX: I'm putting in the first suture.

CHRIS: For 2,000 and more miles in any direction, apart from the tiny bubble of warmth and light in the Antarctic darkness that is the research station, there's nothing but ridges of ice and the occasional bare rock. Around the edges of the ice, there are a few million penguins. And after that, before you even come close to the next human beings, there is the emptiness of the vast Southern Ocean.

JORGE: No need to rush it.

ALEX: I won't.

CHRIS: But even then, she's not alone.

ALEX: How am I doing?

JORGE: It's looking good. Really good.

CHRIS: Outside it's fifty below zero and forecast to become colder.

JORGE: How do you feel?

ALEX: Weak. But I'm okay.

CHRIS: Outside it's sixty below zero, and forecast to become colder.

JORGE: You should lie down.

ALEX: Say hi to my kids for me.

JORGE: I will.

CHRIS: And the woman sat in Antarctica. And she waited, because that's all she could do. She waited for the end of her story. To see how it might turn out.

           And a long way away, a silent radio station came to life. And to whoever might be listening, someone said –

ALEX moves back to lie on the sofa. CHRIS hands JORGE a folded sheet of paper, then sits back at the table. JORGE stays in his armchair, and reads on the mic:

JORGE: Remember the facts.

           These are the facts and these facts will make up the story.

           And the story will be passed on, and people will tell it and they'll say this happened there.

           And they'll mean this is the kind of thing that happens there. In that country. And the story will come to stand for something. It might tell us not just about that country, but something about all of us. If we're lucky.

           But as soon as these things are finished, nobody can really agree what the facts are because they are already in the past.

They will tell the story anyway though. And it will float from head to head. In and out of mouths and ears and newspapers and half-heard conversations in airports, and eventually it might wash up here with us.

And people everywhere will still get born, and still die, and the workings of the internal combustion engine or the speed of light or the taste of those tomatoes will still be the same wherever you go.

And the people in the stories will go on living. Except for the ones who are dead. Because stories never brought anyone back from the dead.

All they are is something to hang on to. For as long as you've got the strength. And it's down to you how long that is. All you can do is grab the stories as they speed past, and see how long they can help you float.

The lights slowly fade to blue, then blackout.

Story Map in progress at Hull Truck Theatre, 2012. Photo: Hannah Nicklin.

Jorge Andrade. Photo: Craig Fleming.

Chris Thorpe in *What I Heard About the World*. Photo: Craig Fleming.

What I Heard About the World at Teatro Maria Matos, November 2010.
Photo: José Carlos Duarte.

**'Consistently innovative and challenging...
extraordinary performances.'**
The Times

Third Angel is a theatre company making entertaining and original contemporary performance that speaks directly, honestly and engagingly to its audience. Established in Sheffield in 1995, by artistic directors Rachael Walton and Alexander Kelly, the company makes work that encompasses theatre, live art, installation, film, video art, documentary, photography and design. The work tours throughout the UK, mainland Europe and around the world, to theatres, art centres, cinemas, pubs, swimming pools, car parks, a public toilet in Bristol and a damp cellar in Leicester.

In 2001 (with *Where From Here*), 2005 (with *The Lad Lit Project*) 2007 (with *Presumption*) and 2013 (with *What I Heard About the World*) the company was invited to be part of the British Council's Edinburgh Showcase. Recent international performances have taken place in Porto, Brussels, Rio de Janeiro, Beirut and Washington D.C.

Third Angel also runs a Participation Programme, which includes delivering Arts Award to young people, free skills workshops for teenagers (*Future Makers*), mentoring emerging and established artists and companies, offering opportunities for aspiring arts managers and technicians, delivering lectures and workshops around the country, and making shows with BA and MA students.

'... engaging with the big issues about how we live with a fierce intelligence.'
The Guardian

'A genuinely brilliant theatre company'
Yorkshire Post

Third Angel is an Associate Company at Sheffield Theatres, and an Arts Council England National Portfolio Organisation.

For more information about our work, online resources and videos, and to join our mailing list, please visit us at: **www.thirdangel.co.uk**

The production of *There's A Room* has been supported by Arts Council England and Leeds Beckett University.

Theatre Pieces

Inherited Cities
2018. Co-production with Sheffield Theatres.

The Department of Distractions
2018. Co-production with Northern Stage, in association with Sheffield Theatres.

Partus
2016. Co-production with Sheffield Theatres.

600 People
2015. Commissioned by Northern Elements / ARC Stockton.

The Paradise Project
2014. Co-production with mala voadora & Teatro Maria Matos.

The Life & Loves of a Nobody
2014. Co-production with Sheffield Theatres.

The Machine
2013. From the radio play by Georges Perec.

What I Heard About The World
2010. Co-production with mala voadora, Sheffield Theatres & Teatro Maria Matos.

All About The Full Stops
2010. Commissioned for *Three* by Queer Up North & Development Lab.

Parts For Machines That Do Things
2008. Co-production with Sheffield Theatres.

Off The White
2007. Co-production with Teatro Praga & Culturgest, Lisbon.

Presumption
2006. In association with Sheffield Theatres.

The Lad Lit Project
2005. Supported by Sheffield Theatres, Leeds Met Studio & Prema.

Stage An Execution
2003. Commissioned by NationalTheater Mannheim.

Leave No Trace
2002. Supported by The Hawth.

Believe The Worst
2001. Supported by The Hawth.

Where From Here
2000. Supported by The ICA.

The Secret Hippie Piece
2000. A collaboration with Drei Wolken for Transeuropa.

Hang Up
1999. Commissioned by Arnolfini Live.

What Happens If…
1999. Commissioned by Leeds Met Studio Theatre.

Experiment Zero
1997.

Performance and Installation Pieces

The Journeys
2017. A collaboration with SBC Theatre, commissioned by Migration Matters Festival.

The Desire Paths
2016. Commissioned by Sheffield Year of Making; supported by Northern Stage.

Cape Wrath
2013. Supported by ARC Stockton & Leeds Beckett University.

Favourite Ever Christmas Present
2011.

Story Map
2010. Co-production with mala voadora.

Inspiration Exchange
2010. Created for Cafe Scientifique.

Words & Pictures
2009. Commissioned by Off The Shelf and Leeds Met Studio Theatre.

Homo Ludens
2009. Co-production with TiG7 for Schillertage and Schwindelfrei.

9 Billion Miles From Home
2007. Commissioned by Chelsea Theatre.

The Expected Lifespan Of Dreams
2006. Commissioned by Site Gallery for Light Night.

Standing Alone, Standing Together
2005. Commissioned by Millennium Galleries, Sheffield,
for the exhibition *Tate Sculpture*.

Palm
2005. Commissioned by home, London.

Hurrysickness
2004. Commissioned by Wonderful & Arnolfini Live.

Pleasant Land
2003. Commissioned by Leeds Met Gallery & Studio Theatre.

Where Have They Hidden All The Answers?
2002. Commissioned by NRLA.

Pills For Modern Living
2001.

Class of '76
2000. Commissioned by Small Acts at the Millennium & Site Gallery.

Saved
1998. Commissioned by BAC/BFVT, NRLA and Performulate.

Senseless
1998. Commissioned by Arnolfini Live & The Mappin Art Gallery.

Shallow Water
1997. Commissioned by The Ferens Art Gallery.

The Killing Show
1996. Commissioned by Lovebytes Digital Arts Festival.

CandleTable, Barcode & Experiment Zero
1996. 3 Quarterlight commissions.

Testcard
1995. Supported by The Workstation & the *northern* media school.

Internet projects, Films and Video Work

The Small Celebrations
2016. New short video pieces by Action Hero, Hannah Butterfield, Massive Owl, RashDash and Third Angel.

Empty Benches & Red Phoneboxes
Photography projects, 2006 onwards.

Happy?
2012. 7 min. HD. Funded by ESRC.

whatiheardabouttheworld.co.uk
2011. With mala voadora.

Mixtape: Songmap
2010. 8 min. HDV. Commissioned by Unlimited Theatre.

Technology
2009. 10 min. DV.

A Perfect Circle
2009. 10 min. DV. Commissioned by The Sheffield Pavilion.

Digital Shorts
1998 – 2005. 5 shorts, 2-5 min. DV.

Realtime
2004. 8 min/loop. DV. Commissioned by Wonderful & Arnolfini Live.

www.pleasantland.org
2003/04. A Shooting Live Artists commission.

On Pleasure
1997. 15 min. S16mm. An LWT Production for *The South Bank Show*.

With The Light On
1996. 19 min. S16mm.

WWW.OBERONBOOKS.COM

Follow us on Twitter @oberonbooks
& Facebook @OberonBooksLondon